Current
CONTROVERSIES

The Global Impact
of Social Media

Other Books in the Current Controversies Series

The Global Impact
of Social Media

Dedria Bryfonski, Book Editor

GREENHAVEN PRESS
A part of Gale, Cengage Learning

GALE
CENGAGE Learning·

Detroit • New York • San Francisco • New Haven, Conn • Waterville, Maine • London

GALE
CENGAGE Learning·

Elizabeth Des Chenes, *Managing Editor*

© 2012 Greenhaven Press, a part of Gale, Cengage Learning

Gale and Greenhaven Press are registered trademarks used herein under license.

For more information, contact:
Greenhaven Press
27500 Drake Rd.
Farmington Hills, MI 48331-3535
Or you can visit our Internet site at gale.cengage.com

For product information and technology assistance, contact us at

Gale Customer Support, 1-800-877-4253
For permission to use material from this text or product, submit all requests online at www.cengage.com/permissions

Further permissions questions can be emailed to permissionrequest@cengage.com

Articles in Greenhaven Press anthologies are often edited for length to meet page requirements. In addition, original titles of these works are changed to clearly present the main thesis and to explicitly indicate the author's opinion. Every effort is made to ensure that Greenhaven Press accurately reflects the original intent of the authors. Every effort has been made to trace the owners of copyrighted material.

Cover image copyright © ildogesto/Shutterstock.com.

LIBRARY OF CONGRESS CATALOGING-IN-PUBLICATION DATA

The global impact of social media / Dedria Bryfonski, book editor.
    p. cm. -- (Current controversies)
    Includes bibliographical references and index.
    ISBN 978-0-7377-5620-3 (hardcover) -- ISBN 978-0-7377-5621-0 (pbk.)
    1. Social media. 2. Social media--Political aspects. 3. Globalization--Social aspects. I. Bryfonski, Dedria.
    HM1206.G563 2012
    303.48'2028567--dc23
                                                        2011026398

Printed in the United States of America
2 3 4 5 6   15 14 13 12 11

FD360

Contents

Chapter 1: Are Social Networks Valid Sources for News?

Kristen Purcell, Lee Rainie, Amy Mitchell, Tom Rosenstiel, and Kenny Olmstead

Most Americans now employ multiple media to get their news, and the Internet is the medium that has been the major change agent. There are three "Ps" that define how people want their news—portable, personalized, and participatory. These trends have been enabled by the popularity of social media sites that enable people to post news that is relevant to them and the development of smartphones that has changed how news is gathered and disseminated.

Yes: Social Networks Are Valid Sources for News

Randi Zuckerberg, as told to Rory O'Connor

Facebook's mission is to enable people to share information that is important to them with their friends. In a world where there is a confusing amount of information available, people rely on these "trusted referrals" from their friends to help filter and make sense of the news.

Michael Skoler

Traditional news organizations have lost the trust of readers, particularly younger people. Younger people don't want to be passive recipients of news. They want information that they can control and that is relevant to their lives. By using social media sites to listen to people and establish a connection with them, journalists can regain relevance.

Chapter 2: What Impact Do Social Media Have on Politics?

Chapter 3: Can Social Media Facilitate Political Change?

Chapter 4: Should People Have Unrestricted Access to Social Networks?

Yes: People Should Have Unrestricted Access to Social Networks

The United States believes in and will vigorously protect access to a single Internet where people worldwide have unfettered access to information and the sharing of ideas. There is a direct correlation between the free flow of information and human progress. Those countries that censor social networks and search engines are denying their citizens a fundamental human right.

Foreword

By definition, controversies are "discussions of questions in which opposing opinions clash" (Webster's Twentieth Century Dictionary Unabridged). Few would deny that controversies are a pervasive part of the human condition and exist on virtually every level of human enterprise. Controversies transpire between individuals and among groups, within nations and between nations. Controversies supply the grist necessary for progress by providing challenges and challengers to the status quo. They also create atmospheres where strife and warfare can flourish. A world without controversies would be a peaceful world; but it also would be, by and large, static and prosaic.

The Series' Purpose

The purpose of the Current Controversies series is to explore many of the social, political, and economic controversies dominating the national and international scenes today. Titles selected for inclusion in the series are highly focused and specific. For example, from the larger category of criminal justice, Current Controversies deals with specific topics such as police brutality, gun control, white collar crime, and others. The debates in Current Controversies also are presented in a useful, timeless fashion. Articles and book excerpts included in each title are selected if they contribute valuable, long-range ideas to the overall debate. And wherever possible, current information is enhanced with historical documents and other relevant materials. Thus, while individual titles are current in focus, every effort is made to ensure that they will not become quickly outdated. Books in the Current Controversies series will remain important resources for librarians, teachers, and students for many years.

In addition to keeping the titles focused and specific, great care is taken in the editorial format of each book in the series. Book introductions and chapter prefaces are offered to provide background material for readers. Chapters are organized around several key questions that are answered with diverse opinions representing all points on the political spectrum. Materials in each chapter include opinions in which authors clearly disagree as well as alternative opinions in which authors may agree on a broader issue but disagree on the possible solutions. In this way, the content of each volume in Current Controversies mirrors the mosaic of opinions encountered in society. Readers will quickly realize that there are many viable answers to these complex issues. By questioning each author's conclusions, students and casual readers can begin to develop the critical thinking skills so important to evaluating opinionated material.

Current Controversies is also ideal for controlled research. Each anthology in the series is composed of primary sources taken from a wide gamut of informational categories including periodicals, newspapers, books, US and foreign government documents, and the publications of private and public organizations. Readers will find factual support for reports, debates, and research papers covering all areas of important issues. In addition, an annotated table of contents, an index, a book and periodical bibliography, and a list of organizations to contact are included in each book to expedite further research.

Perhaps more than ever before in history, people are confronted with diverse and contradictory information. During the Persian Gulf War, for example, the public was not only treated to minute-to-minute coverage of the war, it was also inundated with critiques of the coverage and countless analyses of the factors motivating US involvement. Being able to sort through the plethora of opinions accompanying today's major issues, and to draw one's own conclusions, can be a complicated and frustrating struggle. It is the editors' hope that Current Controversies will help readers with this struggle.

Introduction

"Despite its roots as a US college site, Facebook took the global lead in social networking with more than 70 percent of its users outside the United States as of early 2011."

Facebook was launched at Harvard University in 2004 as a way of linking college students. By the spring of 2011, it had six hundred million users. If its users made up a nation, it would be the third largest in the world. Facebook has been credited by many political commentators as having a role in the election of Barack Obama as US president and in facilitating revolutions in the Middle East. How did Facebook and other social networking sites such as Twitter, MySpace, and LinkedIn get so big and influential so fast? To answer this question, it's helpful to have a brief history of social networks.

Although the growth of social networking sites has been explosive in the first decade of the twenty-first century, social networking has been around in some form since 1971, when the first e-mail was sent. The next step in the evolution occurred in 1978, with the development of the Bulletin Board System, or BBS. A BBS is an electronic system enabling users to exchange messages or download applications and data over phone lines. Most of its users were in the technology field; therefore, the BBS market was considered a niche market.

With the launch of CompuServe and The Source in 1979, online services reached general business and consumer markets. CompuServe eventually gained market dominance by providing Internet connectivity, real-time chat, and electronic mail. In 1984 Prodigy Communications Corporation came along to challenge CompuServe. Prodigy's distinction was its graphical user interface that enriched the user's experience with images rather than straight text. E-mail and message boards were two of Prodigy's most popular applications.

The Internet had been around since the late 1960s, but its popularity skyrocketed in 1991 with the launch of the World Wide Web (WWW or the web). The web was a service that enabled content on the Internet to be linked and connected. America Online (eventually renamed AOL) was launched in 1991 and developed a successful strategy around linking its service to the web. Games and chat rooms became other popular features on America Online, and the service gained a market lead with 23.2 million subscribers by 2000.

In 2002 a new kind of website was launched, one that *Fortune* magazine said was "more about connecting people to people than people to websites." The site was called Friendster, and it grew to three million users within its first three months. Friendster is generally acknowledged to be the first social media site. Its initial mission was to be an online dating site, under the premise that friends of friends would make safer and more suitable dating partners than complete strangers. Friendster was considered a great idea that was poorly executed—the service was plagued by outages and slowdowns—and the field was ripe for competitors to strike. As of June 2010, Friendster had 90 million users, with 90 percent of them in Asia.

Several executives of eUniverse, an Internet-based marketing and entertainment company, were members of Friendster and quickly saw the opportunity to create a competitor. In 2003, MySpace was created and quickly overtook Friendster. With its roots in southern California and the entertainment industry, MySpace attracted artists, musicians, and actors. The site gave the user the ability to connect with others and to create a distinctive web page, a feature that proved especially popular with bands. For a while, MySpace was the leading social network, overtaken in 2008 by Facebook. Commentators pointed to concerns about safety as one of the reasons for MySpace's decline. As of March 2011, it had 260 million users.

In February 2004 Harvard sophomore Mark Zuckerberg launched Facebook as a way of connecting Harvard students. He soon expanded it to other universities, then to high schools. As of September 2006, the site was open to all with a registered e-mail address. In discussing the genesis of Facebook, Zuckerberg talked about his idea to connect Harvard students:

> Six thousand people to share some information about themselves and stay connected with their friends and family. And what we basically just found since then is that that application is something that almost everyone wants to use.
>
> Everyone has an identity that they want to express and friends and family that they wanna stay connected with.

In 2006 another major player in the social media world was launched—Twitter. The three founders of Twitter—Jack Dorsey, Evan Williams, and Biz Stone—wanted to send short messages via their cell phones. A *tweet*, or a message on Twitter, can be no more than 140 characters long. As of spring 2011, there were more than two hundred million people with Twitter accounts, and the service has gained popularity as a way of sending citizen-based accounts of breaking news events.

While MySpace and Facebook are used mostly for social interaction and Twitter is often used to share information, LinkedIn, launched in May 2003, is a business-oriented social network designed to assist people in networking with others in the same field. As of spring 2011, LinkedIn had one hundred million users.

Not only were the popular social media sites growing, they were growing at staggering rates. Twitter and LinkedIn each more than doubled their user accounts from 2010 to 2011, while Facebook grew from 350 million active users to more than 600 million. Facebook overtook Google as the most-visited site on the web globally in 2010. Exponential growth outside the United States fueled this expansion. Despite its roots as a US college site, Facebook took the global lead in social networking with more than 70 percent of its users outside the United States as of early 2011. LinkedIn and Twitter also reported more than 50 percent of their users were from outside the United States. Sree Sreenivasan, digital media professor at Columbia University, in a National Public Radio interview, explained the popularity of Facebook outside the United States:

> Social networks have been around for years. And you take an example of a country like Brazil. In Brazil the biggest social network is something called Orkut, O-R-K-U-T, a Google project that failed in America, but has been so successful that every Brazilian on Earth who's online is on Orkut.

> But in recent months, people are moving onto Facebook. And when you ask them why are you on Facebook, they say Orkut is still important. It's for us to talk to each other. But Facebook is to talk to the world.

Social media became a global phenomenon in less than a decade. The viewpoints of journalists, commentators, and political and social scientists are presented in the following chapters: Are Social Networks Valid Sources for News? What Impact Do Social Media Have on Politics? Can Social Media Facilitate Political Change? and Should People Have Unrestricted Access to Social Networks?

Are Social Networks Valid Sources for News?

Overview: Social Media Make News a Social Experience

Kristen Purcell, Lee Rainie, Amy Mitchell, Tom Rosenstiel, and Kenny Olmstead

Kristen Purcell is the associate director for research at Pew Research Center's Internet & American Life Project. Lee Rainie is the director of the Pew Research Center's Internet & American Life Project. Amy Mitchell is deputy director for the Pew Research Center's Project for Excellence in Journalism. Tom Rosenstiel is the director of the Pew Research Center's Project for Excellence in Journalism. Kenny Olmstead is a research analyst at the Pew Research Center's Project for Excellence in Journalism.

In the digital era, news has become omnipresent. Americans access it in multiple formats on multiple platforms on myriad devices. The days of loyalty to a particular news organization on a particular piece of technology in a particular form are gone. The overwhelming majority of Americans (92%) use multiple platforms to get news on a typical day, including national TV, local TV, the Internet, local newspapers, radio, and national newspapers. *Some 46% of Americans say they get news from four to six media platforms on a typical day. Just 7% get their news from a single media platform on a typical day.*

The Internet Has Changed How People Get News

The Internet is at the center of the story of how people's relationship to news is changing. Six in ten Americans (59%) get news from a combination of online and off-line sources on a

Kristen Purcell, Lee Rainie, Amy Mitchell, Tom Rosenstiel, and Kenny Olmstead, "Understanding the Participatory News Consumer," *Pew Internet & American Life Project*, March 1, 2010. http://pewinternet.org. Reproduced by permission.

typical day, and the Internet is now the third most popular news platform, behind local television news and national television news.

The process Americans use to get news is based on foraging and opportunism. They seem to access news when the spirit moves them or they have a chance to check up on headlines. At the same time, gathering the news is not entirely an open-ended exploration for consumers, even online where there are limitless possibilities for exploring news. While online, most people say they use between two and five online news sources and 65% say they do not have a single favorite website for news. Some 21% say they routinely rely on just one site for their news and information.

News consumption is a socially engaging and socially driven activity, especially online.

In this new multi-platform media environment, people's relationship to news is becoming portable, personalized, and participatory. These new metrics stand out:

- *Portable*: 33% of cell phone owners now access news on their cell phones.

- *Personalized*: 28% of Internet users have customized their home page to include news from sources and on topics that particularly interest them.

- *Participatory*: 37% of Internet users have contributed to the creation of news, commented about it, or disseminated it via postings on social media sites like Facebook or Twitter.

To a great extent, people's experience of news, especially on the Internet, is becoming a shared social experience as people swap links in e-mails, post news stories on their social networking site feeds, highlight news stories in their tweets [posts made on Twitter], and haggle over the meaning of events in discussion threads. For instance, more than 8 in 10 online news consumers get or share links in e-mails.

The rise of the Internet as a news platform has been an integral part of these changes.... [Two significant technological trends have influenced] news consumption behavior: First, the advent of social media like social networking sites and blogs has helped the news become a social experience in fresh ways for consumers. People use their social networks *and* social networking technology to filter, assess, and react to news. Second, the ascent of mobile connectivity via smartphones has turned news gathering and news awareness into an anytime, anywhere affair for a segment of avid news watchers....

Getting News Is Participative

News consumption is a socially engaging and socially driven activity, especially online. The public is clearly part of the news process now. Participation comes more through sharing than through contributing news themselves.

Getting news is often an important social act. Some 72% of American news consumers say they follow the news because they enjoy talking with others about what is happening in the world and 69% say keeping up with the news is a social or civic obligation. And 50% of American news consumers say they rely to some degree on people around them to tell them the news they need to know. Online, the social experience is widespread:

- 75% of online news consumers say they get news forwarded through e-mail or posts on social networking sites and 52% say they share links to news with others via those means.

- 51% of social networking site (e.g., Facebook) users who are also online news consumers say that on a typical day they get news items from people they follow.

Another 23% of this cohort follow news organizations or individual journalists on social networking sites.

Some 37% of Internet users have contributed to the creation of news, commentary about it, or dissemination of news via social media. They have done at least one of the following: commenting on a news story (25%); posting a link on a social networking site (17%); tagging content (11%); creating their own original news material or opinion piece (9%); or tweeting about news (3%).

Facebook Helps People Share Credible Information

Randi Zuckerberg, as told to Rory O'Connor

Rory O'Connor, a documentary filmmaker and journalist, is president and cofounder of the international media firm Globalvision and the Global Center, an educational foundation. While a fellow at the Joan Shorenstein Center on the Press, Politics and Public Policy at Harvard University, he researched the role social media plays in addressing issues of journalist credibility. In the following viewpoint, O'Connor interviews Randi Zuckerberg, the marketing director of Facebook.

*R*ory O'Connor: With slumping public approval, journalism is *facing a crisis of trust. We're looking at how people can find and share credible news and information in hopes of regaining this trust. Do you think Facebook plays a role in this process at all? If so, how?*

News Shared by a Friend Is More Powerful

Randi Zuckerberg: The concept of "the trusted referral" is integral to the success of content sharing on Facebook. We've found that it is tremendously more powerful to get a piece of content—an article, a news clip, a video, etc.—from a friend, and it makes you much more likely to watch, read, and engage with the content.

People will always want to consume content from experts and they will always look to trusted news sources and journalists for important news and current events, but the market has become so oversaturated that it is now just as important to rely on one's friends to help filter the news. When you get a news clip from a friend, they are putting their own personal brand on the line, saying, "I recommend THIS piece of content to you out of all the content that is out there"—just as they would recommend a restaurant, or a movie.

We are beginning to see journalists and news/broadcast companies creating a significant presence on Facebook to engage with Facebook users and help facilitate this notion of the trusted referral to assist with the viral spread of content. When journalists can really engage with this audience and enlist Facebook users to market and share their content, that is such a powerful way to share credible news and information and tap into the implicit trust that people have with their friends.

The conventional wisdom in academia is that social networks do the opposite, they serve as polarizing echo chambers where users reinforce their own views rather than being persuaded to listen and perhaps agree with others. Why or why not does Facebook fit this mold?

This is a great question. I think this greatly depends on where you look within a social website. If you are looking at a user profile, you'd probably be correct in that people use that real estate on the site to build their own personal brand. They post photos of themselves, write about their viewpoints, and tell their friends what they are doing and what they are thinking. So yes, if you look at only the profile, you might believe that social media is just a place for a one-sided posting of information about oneself.

However, if you only looked at the profile, you'd be ignoring a tremendous amount of activity that takes place, on Facebook and other sites. Facebook users join groups to discuss issues, topics, and activities that are important to them. They become "fans" of celebrities, brands, public figures, and businesses. They use applications to see photos of their friends traveling the world, read their friends' blog posts, and keep up to date with news and content.

And most importantly, people use Facebook to learn new things about their friends and the world around them. Our mission as a company is to encourage people to share information that is important to them with their friends. Through the news feed on a user's home page, Facebook users see what their friends are doing, thinking, and talking about. They discover new books, new articles, new videos, new places to visit, and new people to become friends with.

Journalists are only beginning to discover what a powerful tool Facebook can be for their content.

I can't even begin to tell you how many new things I have personally discovered through Facebook and how my Facebook friends have broadened my horizons and introduced me to new things I never would have discovered before. On many days, I hear about the current events because my Facebook friends will post articles and write thoughts about it . . . even before I discover it from a news site. I have discovered new places in the world to visit, have been introduced to new and incredible people, have discovered new music and bands to follow, and have had my views challenged on everything from politics to taste in Broadway musicals.

Facebook Gives Traditional Journalism a New Tool

Journalists are using Facebook in unanticipated ways. What are some of the main trends you have noticed? Are you surprised at these novel applications? . . .

I think journalists are only beginning to discover what a powerful tool Facebook can be for their content. In my discussions with many mainstream media companies, I constantly hear them talk about why they are squeamish about posting their content on other sites—their content is their lifeblood, it's all they have . . . why would they give it away for free on other sites?

However, I see more and more media companies understanding the importance of allowing people to consume content anywhere they want to consume it on the web, not just at the media company's website. As I mentioned before, I don't think expert journalism will go away—people will always want a trusted, expert opinion when it comes to news, politics, current events, and important topics—but people would rather get that content on a site they are already on, like Facebook, rather than traveling off to another site if they are already on Facebook engaging with friends and doing other things.

Social Media Can Make Traditional News Organizations More Relevant

Michael Skoler

Michael Skoler is vice president of interactive media for Public Radio International. He also founded and served as executive director of the Center for Innovation in Journalism at American Public Media.

Journalists are truth-tellers. But I think most of us have been lying to ourselves. Our profession is crumbling and we blame the web for killing our business model. Yet it's not the business model that changed on us. It's the culture.

Mainstream media were doing fine when information was hard to get and even harder to distribute. The public expected journalists to report the important stories, pull together information from sports scores to stock market results, and then deliver it all to our doorsteps, radios and TVs. People trusted journalists and, on our side, we delivered news that was relevant—it helped people connect with neighbors, be active citizens, and lead richer lives.

Advertisers, of course, footed the bill for news gathering. They wanted exposure and paid because people, lots of people, were reading our newspapers or listening to and watching our news programs.

But things started to change well before the web became popular. Over the past few decades, news conglomerates took over local papers and stations. Then they cut on-the-ground reporters, included more syndicated content from news ser-

Michael Skoler, "Why the News Media Became Irrelevant—and How Social Media Can Help: 'Only the Savviest of Journalists Are Using the Networks for the Real Value They Provide in Today's Culture—As Ways to Establish Relationships and Listen to Others,'" *Nieman Reports*, v. 63, no. 3, Fall 2009, pp. 38–40. Copyright © 2009 by Nieman Reports. All rights reserved. Reproduced by permission.

vices, and focused local coverage on storms, fires, crashes and crime to pad profit margins. The news became less local and less relevant, and reporters became less connected to their communities. Surveys show a steep drop in public trust in journalism occurring during the past 25 years.

As discontent grew among the audience, the Internet arrived. Now people had choices. If the local paper and stations weren't considered trustworthy and journalists seemed detached from what really mattered to them, people could find what they wanted elsewhere. What's more, they could stop being passive recipients. They could dig deeply into topics, follow their interests, and share their knowledge and passions with others who cared about similar things.

Connecting Through Trust

The truth is the Internet didn't steal the audience. We lost it. Today fewer people are systematically reading our papers and tuning into our news programs for a simple reason—many people don't feel we serve them anymore. We are, literally, out of touch.

Today, people expect to share information, not be fed it. They expect to be listened to when they have knowledge and raise questions. They want news that connects with their lives and interests. They want control over their information. And they want connection—they give their trust to those they engage with—people who talk with them, listen and maintain a relationship.

Trust is key. Many younger people don't look for news anymore because it comes to them. They simply assume their network of friends—those they trust—will tell them when something interesting or important happens and send them whatever their friends deem to be trustworthy sources, from articles, blogs, podcasts, Twitter feeds, or videos.

Mainstream media are low on the trust scale for many and have been slow to reach out in a genuine way to engage people.

Many news organizations think interaction is giving people buttons to push on websites or creating a walled space where people can "comment" on the news or post their own "iReports."

People aren't fooled by false interaction if they see that news staff don't read the comments or citizen reports, respond and pursue the best ideas and knowledge of the audience to improve their own reporting. Journalists can't make reporting more relevant to the public until we stop assuming that we know what people want and start listening to the audience.

We can't create relevance through limited readership studies and polls, or simply by adding neighborhood sections to our websites. We need to listen, ask questions, and be genuinely open to what our readers, listeners and watchers tell us is important every day. We need to create a new journalism of partnership, rather than preaching.

And that's where social media can guide us. If we pay attention and use these tools, we can better understand today's culture and what creates value for people.

Relying on Collective Wisdom

Today's new culture is about connection and relationship. Social networks are humming because they fit the spirit of the time, not because they created the spirit of sharing. They're about listening to others and responding. They're about pursuing our interests because we know they will converge with the interests of others. The new culture values sharing information and being surprised by the experiences, knowledge and voices of others.

The old journalism, with its overreliance on the same experts and analysts, is out of touch with a culture of information sharing, connection and the collective wisdom of diverse voices passing along direct experience.

Take Wikipedia as an example. For better or worse, most school kids treat it as the first place to go for information, and so do many adults. It's not written by scholars, as is *Encyclopaedia Britannica*, but by citizen experts. In today's culture, collective expertise carries as much or more weight than scholarship or deference to titles. And while fewer than 45,000 people are actively contributing to the nearly three million English articles on the site, people know that anyone can contribute, and they have trust in the culture's collective wisdom.

Digg and Reddit are popular as sites because they are about collective wisdom and trust. These social bookmarking sites help people find relevant news based on who is recommending stories. Anyone can play, even if experienced and dedicated users have an advantage. Twitter is half diary and half stream of consciousness, and it is all about relationships and trust because it is easy to follow people, see if there is a connection, and drop those you don't like.

Changing Journalism's Culture

Social media sites are not doing journalism, though sometimes breaking news shows up there (like when a plane crashlands in the Hudson River). For the most part, they rely on news coverage from mainstream media organizations to produce their value. And these sites are not yet profitable. They are not models for the new journalism. But they do serve the new culture and point to how news organizations must change to be considered relevant and value creating.

Of course, news organizations are rushing onto social networks, adding social bookmark buttons, and creating Twitter feeds at a torrid pace. But for the wrong reasons. You can hear the cries in newsrooms of "we need to be on Facebook, we need to Twitter" as a fervent attempt to win followers and increase traffic on their sites.

Mainstream media see social media as tools to help them distribute and market their content. Only the savviest of journalists are using the networks for the real value they provide in today's culture—as ways to establish relationships and listen to others. The bright news organizations and journalists spend as much time listening on Twitter as they do tweeting.

The new journalism must be a journalism of partnership.

Most of the discussion about the "future of journalism" these days centers on finding the new business model that will support journalism in the Internet age. Yet that is premature. There is no magic model that will save us, if only we could find it. We have no business model unless people need our work to enrich their daily lives and value it highly enough to depend on it.

Unquestionably, we must be creative about designing new models and smart about marketing our work. But a fact of business is that people only pay for what has obvious value to them. Every good business plan starts by explaining how it creates value for the customer.

The problem with mainstream media isn't that we've lost our business model. We've lost our value. We are not as important to the lives of our audience as we once were. Social media are the route back to a connection with the audience. And if we use them to listen, we'll learn how we can add value in the new culture.

The new journalism must be a journalism of partnership. Only with trust and connection will a new business model emerge.

Twitter Helps Reporters Connect with the News

Steve Buttry

Steve Buttry is director of Community Engagement and Social Media for Journal Register Company, a news media organization. He has served as director of Community Engagement for TBD, a local news operation in the Washington, DC, area, as well as editor of the Gazette *newspaper in Cedar Rapids, Iowa.*

I have long been an admirer of Edward Wasserman's work. When I was presenting a series of ethics seminars, Our Readers Are Watching, for the American Press Institute, I frequently recommended Wasserman's *Miami Herald* columns on ethics in a list-serv for participants.

Journalists Need to Understand Their Topics

But his latest work shows how smart people can write stupid things when they don't take the time to learn and understand the topic they are writing about. Wasserman, a professor of journalism ethics at Washington and Lee University, clearly is smart. His thumbnail bio with his columns says he was educated at Yale, the University of Paris [1 Pantheon-Sorbonne] and the London School of Economics.

Apparently that meant Wasserman was so educated he didn't have to learn anything firsthand about Twitter before writing about it. His latest column, "How Twitter Poses a Threat to Newspapers," revealed so much ignorance about Twitter that I knew without looking that he had never bothered to use Twitter. But I looked anyway. It's good journalism to do some research and see if your assumptions are correct.

A quick check using Twitter's "find people" function showed no Edward Wasserman on Twitter. (*Update: Wasserman confirmed in an e-mail response that he has not used Twitter. . . .*)

Twitter does pose some threats to newspapers, though I see it as more of an opportunity. As more and more people get their news from Twitter (and not just because journalists and news sources are Twittering, but from people tweeting as they live the news and from Twitter aggregating tweets as news unfolds) and other social media, newspapers need to use these tools effectively and adjust our print products to this rapidly changing world.

Reporters who are using Twitter often aren't sitting in front of a computer screen in the newsroom. They are out on assignments.

Wasserman Sees the Wrong Threat

But that's not the threat that Wasserman sees from Twitter. Here's the real threat he sees:

> The danger is that Twitter will keep reporters off the streets and in front of their screens, that it will further skew journalism toward seeking out, listening to and serving the young, the hip, the technically sophisticated, the well-off—in short, the better-connected. The people who aren't being heard now aren't sending out tweets.

This is the line that most shows Wasserman's ignorance about Twitter. You can use it when you're on the street. Many of us do use it at our computer screens (where we write our stories and columns, analyze data and do other important research, so computer screens aren't bad journalism tools, as Wasserman implies), but Twitter was actually designed for use as a text-message blogging platform. When you sign up to use Twitter (as Wasserman would know, if he ever had), it encourages you to use it on a mobile device.

Reporters who are using Twitter often aren't sitting in front of a computer screen in the newsroom. They are out on assignments, Twittering to be first (or at least quick) with the news and to connect with eyewitnesses and so on.

And I can't let Wasserman get by with the shot about "further" skewing journalism toward the young, hip and technically sophisticated. Please. Every audit of newspaper content (I have conducted some myself) shows that our content is heavily skewed toward people my age (that's middle age) and older (especially if you don't count sports coverage, where most athletes are younger). Middle age and older is our demographic, both in readership and in content.

As Steve Yelvington [a journalist and media strategist] *tweeted* sarcastically this morning after linking to Wasserman's column:

Journalism is just, like, so totally hip and young already.

Among the many reasons newspapers don't have much audience with people who are young and hip is because our content too often reflects ignorance of the world they live in. Such as this column by Wasserman.

Social Media Cannot Replace Professional News Organizations

Barb Palser

Barb Palser is director of digital media for McGraw-Hill Broadcasting Company.

If anybody out there believes citizen reporting and social media are likely to usurp rather than complement traditional media, that person likely has not attempted to follow a major news story through social media alone. The earthquake in Haiti provides a good opportunity to do just that.

Almost a week after the earthquake hit, the Twitter hashtag #Haiti was still crackling with updates at a rate faster than one per second. At that point, the barrage consisted largely of posts about donation drives and benefits around the world, occasional posts about missing loved ones and a smattering of news updates, many of which were re-tweeted from traditional news organizations such as CNN and the *Wall Street Journal*. There was a tremendous amount of talking going on, but it was impossible to tease out a clear understanding of the story from the cacophony. One could refine the Twitter search geographically or topically, but the results still lacked big-picture context.

Meanwhile on Facebook, a group called Earthquake Haiti had amassed 265,000 members by the Monday after the disaster. The activity was a little less frenetic than on Twitter, with new posts every minute or so, but it was still inherently unstructured. Posts in English alternated with posts in French; heartbreaking cries for help alternated with reflections on

Haiti's troubled history. Individuals who were deeply and personally invested in the story (victims' loved ones, relief workers, journalists) would probably find the motivation to sort through the haystack—but as with Twitter, it's hard to imagine the average news consumer using Facebook as a primary source.

This is not meant to discount the literally lifesaving role of social platforms. Out of the Haiti disaster alone, there were numerous stories of victims and their loved ones for whom such sites were a beacon and a lifeline. But as they exist today, social sites are best at getting a speaker's message out to his or her network of acquaintances as opposed to organizing the message with context and perspective.

The bigger a story, the messier and more difficult it becomes to parse the social content. When an airplane lands in the Hudson, there may be only a couple of cell phone photos or videos and a handful of on-the-scene accounts sent forth on blogs or social networks. In a disaster the size of Haiti, you're looking at thousands upon thousands of individual stories, questions, images, calls for help—not to mention hoaxes and rumors.

Compare that with the coverage provided by traditional news organizations on the same social media platforms. For example, the *New York Times'* @haitirecovery Twitter feed provided a well-curated flow of information, including links to text stories, photo slide shows, video and multimedia presentations. Much of the content came from the *Times*, but there were also links to other sources such as YouTube and CNN. The *Miami Herald*, to name one of many examples, also provided updates on Facebook and Twitter, in conjunction with in-depth web coverage. On YouTube, almost all of the popular earthquake-related videos were posted by traditional news outlets.

Even when it came to connecting individuals, the most meaningful development was Google's launch, supported by news organizations and the U.S. State Department, of a "People Finder" application designed to consolidate several disparate missing persons databases into a central tool.

Looking side by side at an open stream of tweets and a Twitter feed maintained by a professional news organization, it's hard to conceive that they could be competing in the same arena. In fact, they are not. The two are so obviously different that the idea of social media threatening the existence of traditional reporting (or vice versa) seems pretty far-fetched.

If anything, the growth of social media amplifies the need for somebody to sort through the anarchic mass of blog entries, Facebook posts, Twitter updates, YouTube videos and Flickr photos that will follow every major news story in the future. This is a role that professional news organizations could take on, in addition to their central mission of original news gathering.

Following the disaster in Haiti, numerous headlines declared that the value of social media had been proven once again during the crisis. This is true. However, the tremendous amount of work done by journalists to report from the scene, and to keep newspapers and websites robust with information, maps, interactive presentations, databases and relief resources, was no less amazing—though perhaps less novel, since they've been at it for so long.

The Southeast Asian tsunami in 2004, Hurricane Katrina in 2005, the post-election violence in Iran in 2009 and now Haiti's horrific earthquake. . . . With each of these major news events, the benefits of citizen media and social networking become stronger and clearer. And so does the essential role of traditional media.

Twitter Is Often Inaccurate

Herman Manson

Herman Manson is a journalist and the editor of Mark *magazine.*

Twitter's value to breaking news quickly and efficiently is beyond doubt, but the accuracy of the news being reported is far from perfect.

The Pressure to Be First Leads to Errors

This weekend [in July 2010], Twitter was abuzz with the news that South Africa's former national police commissioner, Jackie Selebi, was found guilty of *both* charges he was facing. But the initial buzz on Twitter was wrong, or at least not 100% accurate.

At first it was reported on Twitter that he was found guilty on charges of corruption *and* obstruction of justice. What happened initially was that journalists reporting from the courthouse got the first tweet wrong, which meant all the retweets got it wrong as well. Later, updates indicated he was found guilty of corruption but *not* obstruction of justice.

TV reportedly didn't do much better though, with the ETV news channel apparently having to correct itself after a somewhat confusing (for those who haven't studied law at least) judgment by Judge [Meyer] Joffe. Like Twitter, TV is live *if* it has time to prepare for the broadcast in advance. A debate on the technical details of the judgment has already broken out on Twitter, which isn't helping much to limit the confusion factor. . . .

People in the news business love breaking news. This is why we are arming more and more journalists with the equipment to live tweet and blog major news events. And it is entirely true that newspapers and news sites lag Twitter in breaking news. That is because it takes time to write anything longer than 140 characters, to get it fact-checked, and then, to publish/broadcast it to a wider world.

With Twitter able to deliver news quickly and to a potentially huge audience due to its viral nature, already-pressured newsrooms are under increasing pressure to get content out, and to get it out fast. But few are asking what this is doing to journalistic ethics. For example, can media organisations and journalists delete inaccurate tweets that were posted without revealing they did so?

Usually when removing content from a website or withdrawing a story from a newspaper, the editors would admit that they did so and give reasons behind their decision. This is obviously important for the reading public as it holds the media accountable for what they publish. Nobody likes putting their name to that withdrawal notice. Not only does it mean a journalist messed up; it also means the editors missed a beat as well.

The Professional Code of Conduct Needs Updating

Public relations practitioners are already talking about "breaking" news of an event (staged for commercial benefit) via Twitter. According to the earlier-mentioned info graphic, they would position themselves to serve as "witnesses," in order for their "news" to be happily re-tweeted by the rest of us, and effectively bypassing any editorial scrutiny.

Journalists and media organisations should update their professional codes of conduct to take cognizance of the fact that the way we are reporting news is changing.

Of course journalists themselves are being sidestepped by bloggers, citizen reporters and the like. These are people who have little interest in what is viewed as "old school" media practice. Even journalists would admit to relaxing their own rules for their blogs, Twitter feeds and other inter-web media.

Society isn't always well-served by the media. Some stories never see the light of day because of commercial self-interest or political sympathies. In other instances, journalists become mouthpieces for propaganda.

Social media could potentially help counteract some of these issues. On the other hand, it could also cement them even further by turning critical, thought-provoking voices into 140 character sound bites, typed on the go.

Twitter Connects Only the Young and Hip

Edward Wasserman

Edward Wasserman is Knight Professor of Journalism Ethics at Washington and Lee University in Virginia.

The end began in January 1998, when Matt Drudge broke the story on his blog that linked President Clinton amorously to a young White House intern. At least that's how his scoop is remembered, as a signature moment in the growing dominance of online news.

Except that's not what happened. Actually, Drudge didn't break the intern story because he didn't have the intern story. What he reported was that *Newsweek* magazine had the story but wouldn't publish it.

It seems certain one of two things happened. Either somebody at *Newsweek* was fed up with the magazine's reluctance and told Drudge. That would have been the first time a major story went public after being back-channeled from reporters at a mainstream news organization to an unaffiliated website.

Or *Newsweek*'s own sources got tired of waiting for the magazine to publish the scoop. And they sought out Drudge as an alternative outlet.

Journalists Now Reach the Public Directly

What Drudge's scoop really exemplified was the declining ability of news managers to control the access of their own staffs, or their own sources, to the public.

Today, thanks to the Internet most every journalist in this country can reach independently an audience immeasurably greater than the star reporter on the biggest newspaper or top-rated newscast could a generation ago.

Traditionally, the news business was built, one way or another, on a promise of exclusivity: What we've got you won't get elsewhere. So the idea that a media company's biggest threat might come from its own newsroom is hard for news managers to swallow.

To make them really gag, add Twitter.

Twitter is a dazzling social networking technology that allows you to stay in touch, via brief updates known as tweets, with a vast number of friends, acquaintances and interested strangers as you go through your day. Related software enables you to interact with even broader arrays of people you seek out through particular words in their tweets that suggest they know something you're interested in.

It's easy to see why journalists, who depend on just such networks of informants, find Twitter appealing.

Smarter news organizations encourage this. But it comes at a price. Nurturing these online networks obliges journalists to exchange messages with fans and followers, so the potential is there for staffers to spout off, look bad, spill secrets and give away their journalism.

So like parents with marriageable offspring, news bosses are both pushing forward and pulling back, fearful of looking out of date by reminding their eager staff about the danger of going too far.

In recent months some of the country's prestige press—including *The Washington Post, New York Times, Los Angeles Times* and *Wall Street Journal*—have issued staff guidelines. They urge "common sense:" Avoid talking about things you're covering unless an editor approves. Don't come across as opinionated. Don't get into what the *Post* calls "verbal fisticuffs with rivals or critics."

As the *Post* put its bottom-line concerns, "In general, we expect that the journalism our reporters produce will be published through *The Washington Post*, in print or digitally," and not via blogs or tweets.

Good luck there. Can you have journalists texting messages independently on topical concerns with thousands of people using a medium that's easily shared with millions more and still retain exclusivity? I'd say not only has that horse left the barn, but the barn is burning down.

The danger is that Twitter will keep reporters off the streets and in front of their screens.

Twitter will soon be embraced as no less indispensable to reporters than their phones, but it does carry risk—and I don't mean the loss of control that news bosses worry about. It's the illusion of connectedness.

New Media Make Reporters Less Connected

Technologies never brag about what they don't do; they're too busy wowing us with their tricks to admit to their failings. New media technologies trade on the promise that they truly put you in touch, that they have the power to break the bubble of separateness that the journalist struggles within.

Even e-mail, a primitive technology, is seductive. That's why newsrooms fret over a few dozen harsh e-mails as if they're the voice of "the public," and journalism students think a text exchange with somebody is an interview.

Today's networking technologies are a huge leap forward in connectedness, but they can seduce journalists into swapping one bubble for another kind of enclosure. The real danger of Twitter isn't its power to undermine newsroom authority. Let it.

The danger is that Twitter will keep reporters off the streets and in front of their screens, that it will further skew journalism toward seeking out, listening to and serving the young, the hip, the technically sophisticated, the well-off—in short, the better-connected.

The people who aren't being heard now aren't sending out tweets.

 CHAPTER 2

What Impact Do Social Media Have on Politics?

Chapter Preface

Before there was Barack Obama, there was Howard Dean.

Barack Obama is generally considered the first Internet president. "Were it not for the Internet, Barack Obama would not be president. Were it not for the Internet, Barack Obama would not have been the nominee," maintains Arianna Huffington, editor in chief of *The Huffington Post*.

In early 2007, a relatively unknown junior senator from Illinois met with Marc Andreessen, a board member of Facebook, to ask if social networking tools could enable him to become president of the United States. David Carr of the *New York Times* quotes Andreessen's reaction to his meeting with Obama:

> It was like a guy in a garage who was thinking of taking on the biggest names in the business. What he was doing shouldn't have been possible. . . . He was clearly super smart and very entrepreneurial, a person who saw the world and the status quo as malleable.

Obama added to his campaign new-media experts, including a Facebook cofounder, who used social media sites to fund raise, get out his message, instantly respond to issues, organize volunteers, and engage new voters. Importantly, the Obama campaign used social media to organize at the grassroots level, getting volunteers to knock on doors and make phone calls in their own communities. At the end of his campaign, Obama had almost 2.5 million Facebook friends and close to another million supporters on Twitter and MySpace combined, far outstripping his rival, John McCain, who was late to the social media party. The Obama campaign changed the way politicians seek office, opening up a whole new set of tools to engage voters.

However, Obama learned from an earlier, unsuccessful campaign. Howard Dean, former governor of Vermont, campaigned for the 2004 Democratic Party nomination for president using social media and other Internet-based tools. Even before Facebook was created, Dean was using early social media sites to organize and engage volunteers.

According to a January 2004 *Wired* magazine article entitled "How the Internet Invented Howard Dean,"

> The biggest news of the political season has been the tale of this small-state governor who, with the help of Meetup.com and hundreds of bloggers, has elbowed his way into serious contention for his party's presidential nomination. As every alert citizen knows, Dean has used the Net to raise more money than any other Democratic candidate. He's also used it to organize thousands of volunteers who go door-to-door, write personal letters to likely voters, host meetings, and distribute flyers.

Significantly, by the use of social media, the Dean campaign was able to attract the primary users of social media—young people. However, Dean lost the Iowa caucuses, and the 2004 Democratic Party nomination eventually went to John Kerry. Four years later, many of the methods Dean employed were successfully adopted by the Obama campaign. In the following chapter, journalists and commentators debate the role of social media in politics.

Facebook Has a Permanent Role in Politics

Vincent Harris

Vincent Harris is the founder of Harris Media, an online com-munications firm specializing in political campaigns. He ran day-to-day web operations for Virginia governor Bob McDonnell's successful campaign.

1 41,544.

That is the current number of Facebook supporters of Massachusetts Senator-elect Scott Brown [as of January 27, 2010].

What was a perceived advantage online for Democrats across the country has vanished as Republicans begin to "get" the need to embrace social media as a powerful tool to raise name ID and mobilize supporters. The campaigns of Scott Brown and Bob McDonnell [governor of Virginia] prove that Facebook is the best, and only real necessary tool (although one could argue Twitter) that every campaign should embrace online.

Facebook is free. I've seen campaigns and organizations across the country spend thousands of dollars building cus-tom social-media platforms, or waste money paying a design artist to skin their Ning site to reflect their website's look and feel. These costs are unnecessary. While Facebook may not be the shiniest coin, its functionality and organic user base make its usage far more beneficial than spending time and money having to cultivate support on a unique platform.

Facebook Enables Targeted Messaging

A study in December of 2009 showed that 77% of Facebook fan pages have less than 1,000 fans. The best way to break through the initial 1,000 barrier is a two-fold strategy: e-mail and micro-targeted ads. By sending out a social-media centered e-mail, campaigns can convert their e-mail subscribers into Facebook supporters. Regarding Facebook ads: They are arguably better and more effective than any other online advertising medium because ads are targeted to self-identified supporters of specific key words.

Unlike Google where ads are targeted to search or content key words on a specific site, Facebook ads allow you to identify and target people who are in 100% agreement with your values system, regardless of your ideology. Recently I ran a series of 2nd Amendment ads across northern Virginia (yes, there are gun supporters there). Using Facebook's ability to geo-target cities in the region, and then micro-targeting supporters who self-identify as supporters of pages such as "Guns, Hunting, Deer Hunting, Skeet Shooting, NRA, Ammo, etc.," I was able to deliver pro-gun ad copy specifically to the audience I wanted to reach without having to deliver the message in a more public forum as Google ads require. Facebook also provides automatically generated code for an easily embeddable widget which can be placed on a campaign's website, or in blogs.

Using the "advertise something I have on Facebook" feature, Facebook lowers the barrier to becoming a fan of your politician to a simple click on the ad. Ads can also be used to link externally to a website or landing page. A fantastic idea to score kudos with constituents is to target them on their birthdays with a simple message: "Have a fantastic year and Happy Birthday from your Governor."

Campaigns too often don't take advantage of the ability to harvest e-mail addresses on Facebook. No, you don't have to pay thousands to a developer to build an application. Using the website www.emailmeform.com or one similar, a campaign can embed a form into the FBML application and by a quick change of the wall settings, can ensure that every non-fan visiting the Facebook page will land on an e-mail sign-up. We harvested hundreds of e-mail addresses this way with Bob McDonnell's campaign. Campaigns at every level should be utilizing this tool.

Campaigns are slowly waking up to the fact that a Facebook supporter is an avid fan: someone to cultivate, communicate with, and ask for help from.

Building more complex applications on Facebook such as yard signs, or fund-raising tools are more complicated than the average political staffer could create, but are worth reaching out on pricing to your web developer, especially if you have an active and engaged supporter base on Facebook.

With Bob McDonnell's campaign, we made a decision early to make Facebook the primary social network of the campaign, and it worked. By election night we had more than double the amount of supporters as our Democratic opponent, and were well ahead of both statewide candidates in the more populous New Jersey governor's race. Yes, both Bob McDonnell and Scott Brown had the unique advantage of receiving national attention which was a big lure to Republicans across the country wanting to stay engaged with their campaigns, but without our consistent ad presence on the social network (we spent a little over $8,000), and constantly engaging our supporters through a series of Fan pushes, we would not have gotten there.

Campaigns are slowly waking up to the fact that a Facebook supporter is an avid fan: someone to cultivate, communicate with, and ask for help from. These are not merely names on a computer screen, but real people with real free time to make calls from home or knock on doors in the district.

Since Facebook has built their pages with a simple design template, there is not much a campaign can do to change the look and feel of the page except change the main picture in the upper left corner. Understanding this, the McDonnell campaign changed the main picture about once a week, always with a new graphic reflecting the theme or events of the week. When March Madness rolled around, we had a March Madness themed graphic; when we needed to reach a goal of 20,000 fans, we made one for that, and on and on.

Facebook Is Here to Stay

If not overused, supporter "pushes" are an incredibly effective way that a campaign's Facebook fan base can be helpful online. By updating the status of the candidate, and changing the profile picture to reflect a numerical fan goal, you can engage your base directly and encourage them to invite their friends and family to become fans, thereby increasing the amount of people receiving your message. These "pushes" worked incredibly well on the McDonnell campaign, often doubling our number of supporters (5 to 10k [thousand], 10 to 20k) in a week's time or less. Using a free service called Gabcast, Bob McDonnell was able to communicate directly to his Facebook supporters by calling in via phone and recording an audio update which was easily embedded into a status update and could be played directly on our supporters' newsfeeds. People listened when we posted these, and each update would receive hundreds to thousands of listens.

The McDonnell campaign engaged with its fans daily. By posting articles, videos, event schedules, or volunteer opportunities . . . we were constantly staying engaged. One of the best ways to increase interaction is to encourage supporters to simply "like" a status or event; as this takes a simple click, they're much more likely to engage via this medium than leaving a comment. Concerning comments, politicians are beginning to understand that someone who comments on their Facebook page with a concern should be looked at the same way as someone sending a letter to their district office. In this cycle's Vermont governor's race, the presumptive GOP [Republican] nominee, Lt. Governor Brian Dubie, spends hours each week responding to comments himself, as himself, and has received a lot of positive interaction because of this.

The Brown and McDonnell campaigns both spent time and effort trying to emulate Barack Obama's "myBarack-Obama" unique social network by creating their own versions (Brown Brigade, McDonnell Action). On Election Day McDonnell's Action network had fewer than 2,500 members, with less than 200 actually engaging on the network daily. From glances at the Brown Brigade, the activity on there appears similarly bleak compared to Facebook.

The conclusion is that campaigns should try not to reinvent the wheel when it comes to social media. Fellow e-media entrepreneur David All has been preaching this for years, and is infamous for developing platforms that work with Facebook and Facebook Connect instead of spending resources trying to invent the "next Facebook."

For now it seems there will be no "next Facebook" as its dominance atop America's social media sites is secure. With more than 100 million monthly visitors in the U.S. and a recurring placement as the second most visited website, it is very much here to stay. While campaigns like Scott Brown and Bob McDonnell have the advantage of having monetary resources and national attention, Facebook is something that every campaign can and should effectively engage in.

The Impact of Social Media on Politics Is Fleeting

Julian E. Zelizer

Julian E. Zelizer is a professor of history and public affairs at Princeton University. He is the author and editor of numerous books that examine US politics since the New Deal, including Jimmy Carter *and* The Presidency of George W. Bush: A First Historical Assessment.

The Tea Party has rekindled excitement in the potential of the Internet to nurture mass political movements by using the web to raise money and mobilize man power.

Activists have used many aspects of cyberspace: Facebook pages, Twitter feeds, iPod apps and more to rally their supporters. According to Investors.com, "Democrats and their allies dominated cyberspace for years. Now the political right, with the Tea Party explosion, at the very least is matching the left."

The stories about the Tea Party movement resemble the narrative about Barack Obama's campaign.

Facebook Lacks Local Connection

In 2008, Democrats used cyberspace to the same effect. Relying on what I called "Facebook politics," the Democrats took Republicans by surprise by demonstrating how powerful a vehicle the Internet could be in promoting a candidacy, bringing like-minded citizens together and offering an organizational infrastructure for movement politics.

Yet will this form of organizing work over the long term? Can it sustain a movement after the drama of an election is over?

Julian E. Zelizer, "'Facebook Politics' Is Fleeting," *CNN Opinion*, October 5, 2010, http://articles.cnn.com. Reproduced by permission.

The verdict is still out. Since 2008, President Obama and Democrats have discovered that the kind of movement created by the Internet can be extraordinarily fragile and fleeting. When Obama recently spoke to students at the University of Wisconsin, he implored them not to be apathetic and urged them to return to the world of campaigns.

What makes Facebook politics vulnerable is that it lacks the local element that has always been so crucial to politics.

In doing so, he was acknowledging that the movement created by the campaign had disintegrated since the inauguration. The movement has been largely absent from the policy battles that have shaped his administration, and it lags in the months leading into 2010. Obama's team may still have all the cell numbers that they collected before announcing their vice presidential pick, but few people are answering or texting.

What makes Facebook politics vulnerable is that it lacks the local element that has always been so crucial to politics. The most durable forms of political organization have usually depended on local organizing. During the 19th century, political parties were dependent on a dense bottom-up structure rooted in the strength of local political machines.

After Election Day, party operatives continued to remain in close contact with voters. They worked hard—sometimes through illegal means but very often through policy and straightforward patronage—to retain their loyalty and make sure voters were kept abreast of why their party mattered.

Complex Political Issues Are Trivialized by Social Media

Matt Bai

Matt Bai covers politics for the New York Times *and is the author of* The Argument: Inside the Battle to Remake Democratic Politics.

I've been thinking lately about poor Bob Graham, as decent a man as any who ever entered politics. A presidential hopeful in 2004, the courtly Florida senator, who will be remembered for having the foresight to oppose the invasion of Iraq, was generally dismissed as a little too flaky to be taken seriously, and the chief evidence of this flakiness was his 20-plus years of personal diaries, in which he meticulously recorded the most mundane acts of his daily life: the content of his meals, the color of his shorts or tie, the application of his scalp medication. On the day in 1994 when his daughter Cissy gave birth, Graham noted the precise intervals at which he had watched and then rewound and then returned *Ace Ventura: Pet Detective.* After *Time* magazine published excerpts in 2000, rivals and journalists gleefully whispered that Graham was obsessive-compulsive and just plain weird.

Politicians Are Tweeting Mundane Details

It turns out, though, that the weirdest thing about Bob Graham, at least by the standards of the current moment, is that he recorded all of his arcane privately, without assuming that the rest of the world would be dying to read it. Not so for the politicians who have in recent months fallen madly in love with Twitter, the Internet service that lets you send out constant brief updates on whatever you might be doing at the moment—which, when you come right down to it, is really just a Graham-like diary beamed out to hundreds or even thousands of voyeuristic subscribers. "Made it to DC, next stop baggage claim," Craig Fugate, [President Barack] Obama's choice to run the Federal Emergency Management Agency, tweeted upon arriving in Washington last month [March 2009]. A half hour later, he reported, "No bag—great start in DC, the future of things to come?" Fugate's luggage finally arrived the next morning, about an hour before he dashed off this mini-haiku: "Alice in Wonderland, getting morning star bucks." Which kind of makes you wonder: if the head of FEMA feels that disoriented buying a latte near the White House, what's going to happen during a tornado?

Whatever else Americans may be craving in our politics these days, brevity and immediacy aren't among them.

Some politicians use Twitter—or, in many cases, have their staff members use it—as a vehicle for their daily message or as a kind of running travelogue. ("Back from Belgium," Representative Darrell Issa of California tweeted last month. "They make quite a waffle.") Other politicians have decided that Twitter is a way for us to become immersed in the mundane details of their private lives. The clear leader in this field is Claire McCaskill, Missouri's junior senator, who took up Twitter just before the inauguration. "I get old style crunchy taco, and a chicken burrito supreme & Diet Coke at Taco Bell," McCaskill recently tweeted. "Miss those tostados." Then: "Ok, ok, brain freeze. I know you can only get Diet Pepsi at Taco Bell." Give McCaskill credit: she clearly does the tweeting herself, and she shares both her policy positions and the details of her daily life in a way that can be informative and oddly endearing. And yet at times McCaskill, like just about all devoted tweeters, can sound like Tom Hanks in that movie on the island, jabbering to his battered volleyball so as not to lose touch with his own existence.

Twitter Leads to Oversimplification

However current it may be technologically, Twitter seems somehow out of step in its political sensibility—that is, in the promise of false intimacy between politicians and voters. For much of the last two decades, going back at least to George H. W. Bush's pathetic pork rinds and Bill Clinton's wailing saxophone, American politics was obsessed with the universality of our experience, typified by the enduring cliché of the president with whom you could quaff a beer. It isn't hard to see how this happened: the all-powerful medium of television created a stagnating sameness in the presentation of politics that verged on parody, and voters and the news media sought to pierce the artifice, with savvy politicians doing what they could to oblige. But in this new age of reckoning for all that we've failed to accomplish, voters seem to have tired of what pollsters call the "understands people like me" question. Now, it seems, they want politicians to stop sharing and just govern like adults.

And whatever else Americans may be craving in our politics these days, brevity and immediacy aren't among them. Politics today is already too simplistic and binary, its news cycle more comically truncated and ephemeral than at any time in our history; in the age of e-mail, blogs and smartphones, we seem to react to everything with a kind of frantic, predictable impulse (Tax all the bonuses! Kill all the pirates!) rather than with a longer-term consideration of benefits and consequences. The last thing Washington needs right now is politicians who seek to convey the moment in even shorter slogans and commentators who feel the need to offer their wisdom with even more frequency and glib abandon than they already do on blogs and cable TV.

If Twitter doesn't turn out to be just the latest political fad (like, say, psychographic polling, or Ron Paul), then it just may be the worst thing to happen to politics and its attending media since a couple of geniuses at CNN dreamed up *Crossfire* back in the 1980s. It's not that Twitter doesn't have a value to society. Its ability to spread news (as in the emergency landing of a plane in the Hudson River) or to circumvent repression (as in Moldovan youths organizing protests) has already proved transformative. But not every new mode of communication lends itself to politics, where speed and complexity rarely coexist. The capital might be a better place if it became a Twitter-free zone, a city where people spent more time talking to the guy serving the coffee and less time informing the world that the coffee had, in fact, been served.

Social Networks Enable Quick Collaboration Around Issues

Micah L. Sifry

Micah L. Sifry is a cofounder and executive editor of the Personal Democracy Forum, which covers the ways technology is changing politics. He has also served as an editor and a writer for the Nation *magazine and is the author or editor of four books, the most recent being* Is That a Politician in Your Pocket? Washington on $2 Million a Day.

First Maureen Dowd writes a (justly parodied) silly dis of Twitter, and now Matt Bai, who covers politics . . . offers his own misreading of Twitter's importance for politics. Like many inside the Beltway [Washington, DC], Bai focuses on the handful of DC insiders who have begun using Twitter to share details of their day—some inane, some intimate and some genuinely illuminating. But to him, this is most like former Senator Bob Graham's obsessive compulsive diary-keeping: "just plain weird." He adds, "it just may be the worst thing to happen to politics and its attending media since a couple of geniuses at CNN dreamed up *Crossfire* back in the 1980s."

Twitter Is a Powerful Tool for Activists

I guess some of the smart kids in the mainstream media just refuse to learn something new until you spell it out for them. So here's a note to Matt Bai and the other big-foot journalists who are dismissing Twitter:

It isn't what the politicians are doing with it (99% of them, as Bai points out, are using it as yet one more uni-directional communications tool, tweeting to thousands of followers but following—and interacting with—very few). At best, it's a tool for humanizing some of them when used that way, and while that's barely a big deal it hardly seems as harmful as *Crossfire* was to the national discourse.

It's the usage by networks of politically attentive individuals that is far more interesting. Along with blogs, social networks and other interactive communications tools, Twitter is helping knit together real-time response and collaboration across all kinds of political issues and campaigns.

Just take what we did with Twitter Vote Report, as one salient example. In about three weeks, an all-volunteer, loosely linked network of coders, political activists and journalists came together to popularize the #votereport hashtag, get all the voter-protection groups to add it to their Election Day reporting systems, created robust reporting tools and visualization systems (including iPhone and Android *apps* that collected moving audio reports of people's polling experiences), and the whole thing worked on Election Day. More than 12,000 individual reports came in, NPR [National Public Radio], the *LA Times* and the *NY Observer* were among the mainstream outlets that used the data (which was all free for anyone to work with), and I'm sure hundreds of thousands more heard about the project because so many of the reports were flowing in via Twitter. We also pulled in dozens of volunteers who, behind the scenes, volunteered time on Election Day to monitor the incoming reports and help clean up the data so we could categorize information properly and in some case pass along urgent issues to folks in the vote-protection communities and in the press. It's inspired an effort now in India to use the same methods for a project called Vote Report India, by the way.

Conservatives and Liberals Are Both Using Social Media

Bai also missed what the conservatives are trying to do to build new communications networks around common hashtags like #tcot or #dontgo, and how liberals are also using the platform to galvanize their own communities. The other day, the Sunlight Foundation (which I consult for) conducted a brief push to get folks to tweet the 17 senators who are currently on Twitter to get them to cosponsor S. 482, [Russ] Feingold's bill to get the Senate to file its campaign finance reports electronically (rather than on paper), and within a few hours two of them ([Barbara] Boxer and [Claire] McCaskill) had responded directly, via their Twitter accounts, to announce that they were signing on.

While I agree with Bai that our political discourse has become incredibly atomized and sped-up, I would hardly point the finger at Twitter as the cause of that (Blackberries and online news sites have been around a lot longer). It probably does contribute a little more to the speed-up effect, but I would argue that these other networking effects are of much greater import.

Social Media Can Help Citizens Press for Free and Fair Elections

Asch Harwood

Asch Harwood is a research associate in the Africa program at the Council on Foreign Relations.

On September 15 [2010], Nigerian incumbent president Goodluck Jonathan made his long-awaited announcement to run for the presidency in 2011—on Facebook.

Jonathan's decision to shun traditional press in favor of the social networking site to reach a younger generation represents a new phase in Nigeria's online evolution. Unlike the 2007 elections, politicians and civil society groups have a range of new tools to mobilize supporters. But these are accompanied by various challenges: Mobile phones and social media may be potent forces for getting out the vote, but they can also exacerbate tensions between the north and south, the rural and the urban, those with Internet access and those without it, Muslims and Christians, and the over 250 different ethnic groups that make up the Nigerian population. How can civil society campaigns in Nigeria harness new tools for voter mobilization while also promoting peaceful elections?

Using Facebook to Mobilize Voters

One group, Enough Is Enough Nigeria (EIE), a coalition of Internet-savvy Nigerians, has decided to take a cue from Jonathan in targeting the country's estimated 1.76 million Facebook users. Their goal is to mobilize young people to pressure their government for free, fair, and credible elections—something Nigeria has never had despite more than 10 years of civilian rule.

EIE's centerpiece, the Register, Select, Vote, and Protect (#RSVP) campaign, while originating online, is designed to move people from behind their computers and to the polling stations. According to Gbenga Sesan, an EIE board member and Ashoka fellow, "the plan is to use Tweets and Facebook messages to whip up interest and then have people go out physically to register and vote, and they will then use the same tools to report on their activities so we can create an online buzz that inspires more off-line action."

EIE has already had some success mixing online and off-line strategies, helping to organize two rallies, one of which attracted international attention and thousands of attendees. "For our Abuja and Lagos rallies, mobilization was done via online channels—Blackberry messages, Facebook, Twitter, etc.," says Sesan. "We noticed that when celebrities and respected role models—who would not normally be associated with political activism—tweeted or updated their Facebook status with messages about the rallies, their fans and protégés did the same and that improved the chances of their physical presence."

Nevertheless, using online advocacy to mobilize voters faces significant challenges. For one, campaigns like EIE's depend at least partially on government-provided information, which can be inaccurate. Reuters reports that civil society organization West African Nongovernment Organisation Network has already attempted to map polling stations and found that almost 30,000 of the 120,000 stations listed by the Independent National Electoral Commission do not exist. Dr. Alan Rosenblatt, associate director for online advocacy at the Center for American Progress Action Fund, notes, however, that if EIE leverages crowd-sourcing platforms to task voters "with making sure on election day that they report any incorrect locations and where the actual polling stations are, they can quickly compensate for it."

Digital Divide Poses an Obstacle

Access may be a bigger challenge. Internet and social media in Nigeria remain mostly limited to wealthier, literate, and urban Nigerians, who are disproportionately located in southern states. As Dr. Judith Asuni, a senior fellow at the United States Institute of Peace, notes, "I think the idea of using it [social media] to get the youth discussing politics and getting them to feel that they have some power is a great idea; [however] it is aimed at elite people in a way. . . . We still have to work on the how to get the other youth involved."

Given uneven access to the Internet, one answer may be to capitalize on increasing mobile phone penetration. Yakubu Joseph, a Nigerian civil society activist, attributed a recent upsurge in social networking among Nigerian youths to the fact that "even those without access to PCs are accessing Facebook on their mobile phones. This is a positive development that can be leveraged to promote social networking for electoral awareness."

> *The use of platforms . . . may be one step toward engaging Nigerian citizens with the health of their electoral process.*

The substance of the message promoted on social media and mobile phones, however, is also crucial to whether divisions are overcome or exacerbated. Expressing her fears that cell phones and social media could be used to foment divisions and promote violence in the run-up to the elections, Dr. Asuni says, "This is how people spread positive messages and how people spread rumors." Indeed, this year text messages circulated through religious and ethnic networks in the Middle

Belt region in the center of the country, playing a role inciting violence that left by some estimates 1,500 people dead.

"Apart from using such a social networking platform to promote informed decisions among young people in the 2011 elections, there is a need to sensitize them against electoral violence. The educated youths can easily be reached through such platforms, but the vulnerability of the uneducated should not be discounted in this regard. *I think the campaign should encourage role-modeling and reaching unreached targets,*" says Yakubu Joseph.

Jonathan's use of Facebook and EIE's emphasis on social media to connect and organize Nigerian youth represents a "generational shift," as Dr. Asuni notes; it is the first time that these tools have been widely available to both politicians and civil society during a presidential election in Nigeria. Yet whether they can move voters to action *while at the same time combating ethnic and regional divisions* remains to be seen.

Violence or not, the Nigerian elections are unlikely to be widely viewed as legitimate. The overarching measure of success, then, for civil society, will revolve around the degree to which they are able to get people *caring about the illegitimacy of their elections.* The use of platforms, for instance Ushahidi, to crowdsource election observations may be one step toward engaging Nigerian citizens with the health of their electoral process—as well as an important first step toward improving this process.

Social Media Can Be Used to Spread Hatred

Jelena Maksimovic

Jelena Maksimovic is a contributor at Transitions Online *and a web editor at MTV Adria.*

Social networking sites are now the prime locations for the spread of xenophobic views among Serbian youth.

It has become a truism of political activists that if you want to engage young people in politics you must work through social media. Though hailed as tools designed to increase people's participation in civic life, ultimately leading to social change, social networks, blogs, and Twitter can be used by groups with radically different motives. In Serbia the definitive example is the intense campaign against last fall's Belgrade Pride day, led by several extreme nationalist groups for whom social media are the prime channel of communication.

As right-wing groups threatened to disrupt the gay and lesbian parade, authorities asked event organizers to move it to a less central location, but they refused, instead deciding to cancel it. Many people were dismayed by these events, seeing them as the state caving in to violent extremists.

In recent years, Serbia has witnessed the rise of nationalist right-wing groups, notably Serbian National Movement 1389 (SNP 1389). Alongside its anti-EU [European Union] graffiti and participation in demonstrations against the independence of Kosovo, Internet users know SNP 1389 as one of the most diligent nationalist organizations active in social media.

SNP 1389's Facebook group has more than 8,000 members, many of whom post photos and messages on the page. Hate speech is tolerated by the group's administrators. Ahead of Belgrade gay pride, some discussed how to prevent the parade from taking place. One member wrote on the group's message "wall": "I am concerned that they [gay and lesbian rights supporters] have organized themselves so well and that we will not be able to approach them, as the cops will seal all the access points. If the 'faggot ball' goes ahead without any trouble, it will be a huge problem for us. As far as I know, 'our forces' have not organized anything."

Extremists' Backers Remain Obscure

Hired by Belgrade Pride organizers to assess the security risks around the event, Zoran Dragisic, a professor at Belgrade University's Faculty of Security Studies, analysed the websites of SNP 1389 and Obraz, another prominent nationalist group. He found that they make no attempt to conceal their agenda.

"Their ideology is always accessible, as they are using similar tools to those utilized by groups engaged in political terrorism. Their motives are always transparent," he said.

When the two organizations' leaders were arrested after they led their supporters to the location reserved for Belgrade Pride on the day planned for the parade, they instantly became rebels to be revered by a growing number of supporters. The number of "fans" on the SNP 1389 Facebook page tripled from 600 to 1800 when leader Misa Vacic was sent to jail for 30 days on a charge of disturbing public order. Group members posted his "letters from prison" as a blog and on Twitter.

Grassroots initiatives have long been considered the domain of liberal youth. Following Kosovo's unilateral declaration of independence in 2008, a short-lived, informal group known as Biro began producing videos as a backlash against the Belgrade government's myopic focus on Kosovo. Videos such as "I Am Not Your People Kostunica," distributed on YouTube, addressed to the then-prime minister, voiced concern that Serbia was returning to its nationalist past, putting social and economic reforms on the back burner.

One of the founders of Biro, Vladimir Milovanovic, brands these activities as "emotional activism," explaining that at the time he "felt that things were distorted and that such a perception of reality was not good for the society and me, as a part of that society." However, the group soon saw the limitations of YouTube activism as, according to Milovanovic, "The paradox lay in the fact that more than 1,000 people wanted to participate in our activities, while not a single foundation wanted to help us financially."

That view backs up the feeling among many activists that although social media are ideal tools for mobilizing many people quickly, in the long run civil activism still must be sustained in the time-tested ways. The financing of nationalist groups remains a murky area in Serbia. Security expert Dragisic sees a clear link between the state, which was reluctant to protect the Pride participants, and extremist groups.

"These groups are the tip of the iceberg; they appear in the form of a dislocation of power from state institutions. Organizations like these can now prevent any public gathering from taking place. But their leaders are both financially and intellectually incapable of organizing such forceful movements," he said.

Although conclusive evidence is lacking, many Serbian journalists and analysts believe that elements of the Milosevic-era [referring to Slobodan Milosevic, the former president of Serbia and Yugoslavia who was charged with crimes against humanity] secret police remain in place in state bodies, from where they use their influence to support extreme nationalist organizations.

Facebook Wars

Serbian authorities have hardened their public attitude towards extremists since the uproar surrounding the cancellation of Belgrade Pride in September [2009], announcing a closer watch on the activities of extreme nationalist groups, as well as football hooligans. Although ahead of the event State Prosecutor Slobodan Radovanovic had dismissed the threats to gays and lesbians (graffiti in central Belgrade warned, "We are waiting for you"), as "polemics," after it was cancelled he announced that all activities of extreme nationalist groups would be investigated and that such groups would be banned if their activities were shown to be unconstitutional.

Perhaps emboldened by their success in stopping the gay pride parade, nationalist groups then returned to one of their main battlegrounds—stopping Serbia's integration into Western institutions. For most Serbs, the most tangible evidence yet of the country's closer ties to the EU came on 19 December [2009] with the end of the visa requirements for travel to the Schengen area, a step that the government headed by Prime Minister Mirko Cvetkovic had made a priority when it took office 18 months ago [July 7, 2008].

Under the guise of free speech, nationalist and extremist groups are using all available tools to mobilize their supporters and recruit more members.

Nationalist rhetoric kept on hammering on favourite themes such as the preservation of Serbia's historic territory, including Kosovo, the notion that the EU will require Belgrade to recognize Kosovo's independence as a condition for accession, or that joining NATO [North Atlantic Treaty Organization] is also a prerequisite. On 12 January [2010] 200 people, including academics, public personalities, journalists, and politicians, urged the government to call a referendum on Serbia's potential candidacy for NATO. Similar topics occupy the blogs and Facebook pages of nationalist groups.

The SNP 1389 blog lists reasons against Serbia joining the EU: instead of inflammatory language, it features complaints about the "democratic deficit," how the union is led by unelected bureaucrats "known for inefficiency and corruption," and the "useless and expensive" European Parliament.

Alongside the more active groups such as SNP 1389 and Obraz, others, not outwardly extremist, but with nationalistic content, are present in all former Yugoslav countries and are in a "Facebook war" with one another. Their main goal is to accumulate as many supporters as possible for causes such as "Thank God I'm Croatian" (about 10,000 members), "Let's See How Many Serbs Are on Facebook" (more than 145,000 members), and "Group for Abolishing Republika Srpska and the Federation and in Support of a United Bosnia and Herzegovina" (11,000 members). Most are not very active, but the content of the Serbian groups, typically proclamations that Kosovo is still part of Serbia, calls to uphold traditional values, as well as homophobic statements, should be taken seriously as an indicator of the prevailing sympathies of a sizeable part of Serbian youth.

As in many countries, Facebook is the most popular website among Serbian youth, research conducted in 2008 by the international journalism support organization IREX showed. Another unsurprising finding was that the Internet has primacy over newspapers and TV among young people. Under the guise of free speech, nationalist and extremist groups are using all available tools to mobilize their supporters and recruit more members. Their ideology is reflected both in social media aimed primarily at young people and in news stories in popular tabloid papers, known as a buttress of illiberalism in Serbian society since the wars of the 1990s.

In order to counteract the influence of hard-line nationalist views among youth it's necessary to start with the schools, says Marko Karadzic, the state secretary in the Ministry for Human and Minority Rights and one of Serbia's most vocal proponents of the rights of people outside the mainstream of society.

"There is a wider problem of young people's education. Their teachers are not instructed on how to promote tolerance among the students," Karadzic said in a discussion after the screening of a documentary film on nationalist groups. "If we don't change that, physical bans of these groups will be futile."

Political divisions in Serbian society are played out in the online sphere and are engaging not just supporters of nationalist movements. Biro's Milovanovic says he notes something he calls "civic fascism," where "people who stand for liberal ideas are compelled to engage in discussions with people with different political opinions in a banal and vulgar way. The ideology is not crucial here. There is aggression, anger, and discontent on all sides."

Social Media Enable Lawmakers to Communicate with the Public

Colleen J. Shogan

Colleen J. Shogan is assistant director of the Congressional Research Service.

Technological advances have precipitated several recent developments in congressional operations. Perhaps the most significant phenomenon of the past decade is the widespread use of e-mail, which has dramatically altered how congressional offices function. Not since the first live television broadcast of House and Senate floor proceedings has Congress experienced such significant changes to its basic operations. E-mail sparked a revolution in the way that members of Congress communicate, both among themselves and with their constituents.

Technology Alters the Way Congress Operates

Longitudinal statistics concerning constituent mail are available. The last year without widespread e-mail use in Congress was 1997. That year, the House and Senate received approximately 30.5 million pieces of posted mail. By 2007, postal mail had dropped to 18.6 million pieces. However, e-mail traffic for both the House and Senate totaled close to 473 million in 2007. The grand total for 2007—for both e-mails and postal mail for Congress—was 491.6 million. In 10 years, Congress went from receiving 30.5 million pieces of communication to

Colleen J. Shogan, "Blackberries, Tweets, and YouTube: Technology and the Future of Communicating with Congress," *PS, Political Science & Politics*, v. 43, no. 2, April 2010, pp. 231–233. Copyright © 2010 by the American Political Science Association. All rights reserved. Reproduced with the permission of Cambridge University Press.

491.6 million. That is a significant development, and it has profound implications for how Congress functions as an institution.

Technology has also changed how members communicate with each other. The House now has an electronic "Dear Colleague" system that enables members to send communications to other members about proposed legislation, committee action, briefings, events, chamber procedural changes, administrative activities, and other issues. In 2003, when an e-mail-based Dear Colleague system was created, a little over 5,000 Dear Colleagues were sent. In 2007, over 12,000 such communications were recorded. In 2009, a centralized web-based Dear Colleague system went into use, making it even easier to distribute such communications. Over 17,000 Dear Colleagues were issued in 2009.

On the heels of the e-mail revolution, Congress is currently being affected by the proliferation of a relatively new technology—social networking websites. After decisions by the Committee on House Administration and the Senate Rules and Administration Committee, members of Congress are now able to use social networking sites such as Twitter and Facebook, and on their official websites they can post links to YouTube. Members have used these new tools in different ways, and several are pushing the envelope.

For example, one House member hands visitors to her office a slip of paper with her YouTube address. They are informed that their meeting will be filmed, and may appear online. Visitors are also invited to tape their own 30-second spots, which are posted on YouTube. A recent YouTube entry televised the farewell party for the departing interns, culminating in the singing of "For He's a Jolly Good Fellow," with the congresswoman urging viewers to "come intern with us."

In another example, a House member recently experimented with "crowdsourcing," turning to the public to redesign his congressional website. Once finalists were selected, his constituents, along with a web vendor, chose the winning design, which became the member's new official House website. In the press release announcing the winner, the member stated, "Instead of viewing the public as a customer, I believe that we should empower citizens to become our partners in shaping the future of our nation."

Social Networks Possess Great Potential for Change

Social networking websites possess the greatest potential for changes in constituent communication strategies. In particular, I wanted to know how members of Congress collectively used Twitter, which is among the most widely trafficked social networking websites. To do this, I coded every individual message, or "tweet," registered by a member of Congress for two non-successive weeks from late July 2009 through mid-August 2009. I followed a total of 158 members, which included 31 senators and 127 representatives. The data collection resulted in a total of 1,187 tweets during the two weeks. Out of the 1,187 tweets, I found that 828 originated from House Republicans—which is 69.8% of the total. House Democrats issued 166 tweets collectively, amounting to 14.0% of the total.

The tweets were also categorized to determine how members used Twitter as a mechanism to communicate with constituents and the general public: of the 1,187 tweets, 557, or 46.9%, either provided links to other websites or called attention to media activities of the member, such as being on a radio or television show; 298, or 25.1%, described an official action the member had taken on the floor, in committee, or as part of his or her representational duties; and 147, or 12.4%, were position-taking messages. Only 17 of the tweets, or 1.4%, were direct replies to other tweets.

As the minority party, Republicans currently use Twitter more frequently. Not only did more House Republicans use Twitter than their Democratic counterparts, they also tweeted more frequently. House Republicans, who constitute 54% of members registered with Twitter, sent approximately 74% of all tweets during session and approximately 64% of tweets during recess. Despite the partisan disparity in the House, there is no substantive difference between the frequency of tweets of Senate Democrats and Republicans.

Along with other social networking websites, Twitter provides a new set of data for congressional scholars to examine and consider. As of September 30, 2009, approximately 38% of all members are on Twitter, and the number continues to grow. Additional examinations might consider why some members participate in social networking websites while others do not. Further analysis might also determine the effect of Twitter and other similar websites on members' representational behavior and constituent expectations of such duties.

A Two-Way Dialogue May Emerge

It is more difficult to answer how congressional operations will transform in the future as technology becomes an increasingly integrated component of American life. The technological developments discussed earlier have one common element: They all potentially alter the way in which many members communicate—either with each other or with their constituents. This means that technology may change how members engage in their two most basic functions—as architects of national policy and as representatives of their constituents. As technology enables more frequent communication with constituents, one might imagine that the trustee model of representation will wither. If members hear more frequently and loudly what their constituents want, it might become difficult for them to vote in opposition without suffering electoral consequences.

As access to technology widens, congressional staff responsibilities may shift to handle an even higher volume of constituent communications. Consequently, it may become challenging for staff in a personal office to focus on anything but the responses to those who live in the member's district or state. Those who were hired to work on policy might find the majority of their day is spent answering constituent communications. Over time, this might mean that policy expertise will become progressively concentrated within committee staffs and leadership offices. Also, we may see a greater reliance on outside policy expertise, including think tanks, lobbyists, and, of course, the Congressional Research Service. This trend already exists on Capitol Hill, but a wider dissemination of existing technologies and the advent of new crosscutting technology could intensify this development.

More interactive dialogue between members and constituents would likely produce models of policy making quite different from current standards.

In addition to multiplying the volume of messages sent by constituents to their representatives in Congress, changes in technology may eventually facilitate a two-way dialogue. Right now, most of the information still flows in one direction. For example, some members use Twitter or other social networking websites to transmit information about their official actions or policy positions to the general public. There are fewer examples of technology enabling the transmission of information or facilitating a dialogue about policy making or pending legislation that encourages a back-and-forth exchange. This was evidenced by the data collected from Twitter; only 14 tweets of the 1,187 were replies to other tweets.

Members of Congress are likely aware that technology has largely facilitated a one-way transfer of information and ideas. But some members are now experimenting with electronic town hall meetings, which enable the representative or senator to exchange ideas with constituents, even when they are physically in Washington, D.C., rather than at home. There have also been limited experiments with some members asking constituents to contribute ideas or participate in drafting sessions on proposed legislation via web-based applications. Nonetheless, even the most technologically savvy members of Congress may still be cautious about relying too heavily on technology to facilitate communications with their constituents due to concerns about the widespread availability of access to the Internet.

These concerns may disappear in the next decade or two. At a recent technology conference in Europe forecasting the digital revolution in 2030, one expert predicted that the cost of Internet access and wireless devices will drop significantly in the future, enabling comprehensive usage. If this is true, the barriers that currently exist for members to communicate virtually with their constituents may diminish greatly in the future.

Constant communication requires constant work.

Some Devices Are Banned on the Floor

More interactive dialogue between members and constituents would likely produce models of policy making quite different from current standards. For example, the "iron triangle" of power, with focal points residing in congressional committees, interest groups, and the executive branch, might need to develop into a four-sided structure to incorporate direct input and pressure from the public. Interest groups could see their influence weaken as members rely on technology, rather than lobbying intermediaries, to receive information from constituents and mobilized public groups.

Although technological developments have the power to change the behavior of members and how Congress operates, it is worth mentioning that there are still some institutional traditions that refuse to bend. The best example is the ban on laptop computers on both the House and Senate floors. Despite floor use of laptops by members of state legislatures across the country, both houses of Congress have refused to allow members to bring computers with them to their respective chambers. In addition, the Senate does not allow use of Blackberries on the floor, either by members or staff. While cellular phones are banned in the House, the use of Blackberries to send and receive e-mails is permitted. Within the next decade, it is hard to predict whether the use of computers and Blackberries will be allowed in both chambers. However, if social networking websites and other electronic communications continue to play a bigger role in the fulfillment of a member's representational duties, the demand to allow laptops and personal electronic devices will become louder and broader.

The last observation I will make about the impact of technology on Congress is that constant communication requires constant work. The age of Blackberries, cell phones, and Twitter means that members and staff are expected to respond to questions and negotiations outside regular office hours. A former colleague of mine in the Senate slept with her vibrating Blackberry under her pillow. Most people cannot keep up that pace for very long. It is generally accepted that the tenure of Hill staff has gotten shorter, and turnover has increased. Additional reliance on technology and the perpetuation of the "24-hour workday" will likely encourage such trends to continue.

One thing is certain—technology will continue to evolve, and as it does, it will surely affect how Congress operates. In particular, for those of us who provide professional policy analysis for Congress, the role that technology plays will likely affect how we deliver our products, the level of demand for such expertise, and the speed in which we deliver it. At the very least, those currently involved in congressional policy making who want to remain relevant in the future must pay attention to these key benchmarks.

Social Media Pose Risks for Politicians

Kiera Haley

Kiera Haley was an editorial intern at Newsweek *and is currently a copy assistant at Random House.*

Communication is a currency in Washington, a town that maintains its relevance by driving a finely tuned message. Invested right, it pays dividends. But a poor decision can derail months of hard work. For decades, it was prescribed: decide on a message, hold a press conference or distribute a press release, then hope some news outlets put your name favorably in print or on the air. But then social media arrived on the scene, and suddenly all bets were off. Pols [politicians] realized they could amass followers, break news, and hammer a list of talking points on their own terms. Just ask Sarah Palin, the former GOP [Republican] running mate, who, after deriding unfair treatment in the press, found a large following on Facebook and Twitter.

Social Media Encourages an Emotional Reaction

Theoretically, the happy outcome for politicians is a breaking of the mold of traditional info dissemination, the ability to control their own message. But some politicians would be better off if they didn't have complete control. Earlier this summer [in 2009], Rep. Peter Hoekstra fired off a seemingly innocuous line on Twitter in response to the election protests in Iran. "Iranian twitter activity similar to what we did in the House last year when Republicans were shut down," he wrote, in reference to a year earlier when Speaker Nancy Pelosi concluded a House session without Republicans. The line dominated the news that day and opened Hoekstra up to unflattering attacks of faux self-importance and a glib understanding of the situation overseas. California Gov. Arnold Schwarzenegger also got a wake-up call to the raw nature of the new medium after a web video of him wielding a butcher knife to emphasize the need for budget cuts garnered more shock than amusement.

In a media environment where politicians feel the need to instantly have an opinion about everything, the effect is less inhibition to express those opinions. "The instant nature of [social media] encourages people to express the emotion of the moment rather than considering more carefully what they think," says Larry Sabato, director of the University of Virginia's Center for Politics.

Compared to verbal cues, the basis for nonverbal communication originates in a different part of the brain. According to Alton Barbour, author of *Louder than Words: Nonverbal Communication*, the way we communicate with people is based on interpreting a combination of body movements and facial expressions. Raising eyebrows and turning the corners of the mouth can help convey meaning, and emotion, but on platforms like Twitter and Facebook, it's harder to gauge exactly how a thought might be received. "Unless you are skilled as a writer, often people use these media to say things that they think are funny and readers misinterpret because there's a communication that is missing," says Internet psychologist Charles Graham. It also draws back to inhibition. A study of college students in 2008 discovered that nonverbal online-based communications made people more comfortable asking questions or expressing opinions.

There Are Upsides to Social Media

But what's good news for college students can be risky business for pols with a much bigger audience and their jobs constantly on the line. Earlier this year, Virginia Republican Party chairman Jeffrey Frederick fired off a celebratory tweet about convincing a Democratic senator to switch parties that would have shifted the balance of power in the state Senate. "Big news coming out of Senate: Apparently one dem is either switching or leaving the dem caucus. Negotiations for power-sharing underway," he wrote. But the papers had not yet been signed to make the deal official. Frederick's line was picked up by Democratic leadership, who quickly convinced the senator to stay put and subvert the coup.

Other viral faux pas? Scheduled to make an announcement the following morning about whether he'd run for Senate, Utah Attorney General Mark Shurtleff tweeted the night before that he was, in fact, entering the race—a line of less than 140 characters that largely deflated his big next-day press conference. Sen. Claire McCaskill, a prolific tweeter, also had some apologizing to do after revealing a lunch meeting between Senate colleague Michael Bennet and a reporter after another reporter was told Bennet was too busy.

With the inherent risks of micro-blogging and social media, it's easy to forget the upsides too. Openness and transparency can convey an air of frankness, a rare quality among those whose jobs depend on them staying on message. "The more open and honest [politicians] are and the more we see the real politician, the more likely they will get support, since they are the least-trusted of professions," says psychologist Graham. Still, one could argue that if they can't control their typing fingers or the rawness of their sentiments, they probably shouldn't be self-publishing in the first place. It draws back to forward thinking, Sabato says. "One thoughtless comment could turn into the TV ad that beats you in the next election."

CHAPTER 3

Can Social Media Facilitate Political Change?

Chapter Preface

During the 2011 Egyptian revolution, the following joke was being told on the streets of Cairo:

> Mubarak goes to heaven where he meets former Egyptian presidents Gamal Abdel Nasser and Anwar el-Sadat. "What was the cause of your death, poison or assassination?" they ask. Mubarak replies, "Facebook."

A joke, yes, but also recognition of the role that social media had in changing the political order in the Middle East. Revolutions are often sparked by events that cause long-simmering resentments to boil over into action. The Boston Tea Party, for instance, was a tipping point for the American Revolution, as was the storming of the Bastille for the French Revolution. In the revolt occurring in Egypt in the winter of 2011, a Facebook page publicized police brutality and provided a catalyst for activism.

Although commentators and journalists debate the ultimate role social media had in the Middle Eastern revolutions occurring in early 2011, virtually all agree that social media played an important role in publicizing and fomenting outrage over the death of Khaled Saeed (also known as Khaled Said). Saeed was a young Egyptian businessman who was beaten to death in June 2010 by two policemen he had videotaped making a drug deal. Within a few days of Saeed's death, Google marketing manager Wael Ghonim anonymously created a Facebook page entitled "We Are All Khaled Said," which contained the video Saeed had made along with a photo of his battered face. The video was also loaded on YouTube with a message in Arabic urging people to protest police brutality. The video has been viewed more than half a million times, and the Facebook page gained close to five hundred thousand friends within six months.

According to Spencer Ackerman in "Trolls Pounce on Facebook's Tahrir Square," in *Wired*, February 4, 2011,

> "We Are All Khaled Said" is an organizing hub. The administrator explained how to use text messaging to spread word of the protests. It hosted advice on how to avoid police crackdowns and announced where mobile dissident meeting places were. Before this month's revolution emerged, the page taught people how to organize their friends and arranged flash mobs across Egypt demanding change.
>
> Perhaps most importantly, for months it raised peoples' consciousnesses.

As a result, media from the *New York Times* to Al Jazeera credited the Facebook page with a significant role in the rebellion that overthrew the government of Egypt. In the following chapter, commentators and journalists debate the impact of social media on political activism.

Social Media Empower People

Simon Mainwaring

Simon Mainwaring is a branding consultant, advertising creative director, blogger, and speaker. He has been a creative director at Wieden + Kennedy, and he is the founder of the social branding consulting firm We First.

Hundreds of thousands of Egyptians, many wearing bandages from days of street fighting, turned out in Cairo's Tahrir Square on Friday [February 4, 2011] for what they are calling the 'Day of Departure', a nationwide call for the immediate removal and prosecution of Hosni Mubarak who has ruled the country for 30 years. This story is now larger than Egypt and the Arab world, as international news coverage and social media has broadcast the escalating violence around the world, time and again featuring Egyptian citizens dying and risking death in order to have their message heard and for regime change to become a reality. Egypt is widely considered the litmus test for what will happen in the rest of the Arab world, but the importance of social media in its political transformation is larger than that. The use of social media in Egypt is a dramatic demonstration of a clash of cultures; of the old and new, of violence and peace, of the old and young, of the past and future. Or a noted Egyptian blogger Sandmonkey wrote in a tweet from Tahrir Square today [February 4, 2011]:

> One group is peaceful and uses technology, the other is violent and uses rocks to smash your head. Which side do u wanna take? #jan25

Technology Has Matured with Its Users

Malcolm Gladwell, author of *The Tipping Point, Blink* and *Outliers*, questioned the activist value of social media in the *New Yorker* in late 2010 asserting that social media are ineffective tools for serious social transformation. His much-debated article, entitled "Small Change: Why the Revolution Will Not Be Tweeted," argued that social media creates little more than "weak ties" between people warning, "Weak ties seldom lead to high risk activism." By comparison, Gladwell cited the activism of the civil rights movement of the 1960s, which required considerable mental strength and mutual commitment among the groups of black protesters who staged restaurant sit-ins and protest rallies, often under threats of violence and even death. Gladwell maintains this position in regard to the protesters in Egypt and Tunisia writing:

> Surely the least interesting fact about them is that some of the protesters may (or may not) have at one point or another employed some of the tools of the new media to communicate with one another. Please. People protested and brought down governments before Facebook was invented. They did it before the Internet came along.

Social media provides a complex and deep infrastructure perfect for the activist processes of social transformation.

Despite Gladwell's disinterest, the courage of protesters in China (over the suppression of the Nobel Prize winner Liu Xiaobo), Yemen, Tunisia, Egypt and Jordan, to face violence and then share their story using social media is important because of the infinitely scalable connectivity it enables. While Gladwell is right to assert that social media is largely used to exchange trivial information, it is a mistake to limit its transformative potential to the worst excesses of its current practice, denying that technology and the dynamics it enables will mature and grow along with its users, especially in dramatic circumstances such as the protests in Egypt.

Social Media Enables Activism

So to answer critics such as Gladwell and *Foreign Policy* writer Evgeny Morozov, here are six levels of activist empowerment social media enables:

1. One-to-one interaction between individuals connecting via Facebook, SMS [Short Message Service], or Twitter, irrespective of time, distance, or delay. As Clay Shirky writes:

   "We are living in the middle of the largest increase in expressive capability in the history of the human race. More people can communicate more things to more people than has ever been possible in the past, and the size and speed of this increase . . . makes the change unprecedented."

2. Groups of people use social media to form communities, congregating around shared values, whether they are focused on a politician, cause or brand, such as we see in Egypt.

3. Connections between people across platforms, as conversations around shared values and ideas migrate tirelessly from one network to another and amongst different groups. As Henry Jenkins, author of *Convergence Culture*, wrote in response to Gladwell's . . . understanding of social media:

   "We do not live on a platform; we live across platforms. We choose the right tools for the right jobs. We need to look at the full range of tools a movement deploys at any given moment—including some old-fashioned ones like door-to-door canvassing, public oratory, and street corner petitions, to understand the work which goes into campaigns for social change."

4. Dialogues that go on between governments and citizens, or between brands and their consumer communities, using social media.

5. Interactions between the private sector, governments and nonprofits, often with consumers or citizens as intermediaries.

6. The commingling of the virtual and real worlds through the parallel universes constructed within social games and virtual worlds. For example, the use of virtual goods within Zynga's FarmVille game on Facebook to raise funds for earthquake victims in Haiti.

By offering these six levels of engagement, social media provides a complex and deep infrastructure perfect for the activist processes of social transformation—which include information acquisition, knowledge development, transfer and sharing; ideation and thought leadership; empathy and emotional connection; and the spread of credible ideas that inspire cognitive dissonance. These tools are accessible to everyone, available 24/7, infinitely scalable, real time and free. As Twitter cofounder Biz Stone succinctly wrote in response to Gladwell's article, "Lowering the barrier to activism doesn't weaken humanity, it brings us together and it makes us stronger."

As more people use social media to tell the story of the future, the wants and needs of more people will be reflected. Like all technology, social media is neutral but is best put to work in the service of building a better world. This week that involves the tragic loss of so many lives in Egypt as its citizens take to the streets to draft a new chapter in the their history. Their courage, sacrifice and story should not be dismissed or undervalued for in the mutually dependant global community we now live in, or what I call a We First world, their story is our own.

The Tunisian Revolt Was the World's First Facebook Revolution

Anshel Pfeffer

Anshel Pfeffer covers military, international, and Jewish news for Haaretz.com, an Israeli, English-language news website.

Alarge crowd gathered in Tunis' crowded airport terminal Tuesday afternoon [January 18, 2011] around Moncef Marzouki, the opposition leader who had just returned from exile. Sufian Belhaj stood to the side, observing with a small smile. Only when the crowd began to disperse did he walk over and introduce himself to lawyer Radya Nasrawy, a veteran human rights activist. When he introduced himself, using the name he had been using over the past two months, she smiled broadly and kissed him on both cheeks. Online he is known as Hamadi Kaloutcha, and his real identity had been secret until last week, when police officers in civilian clothing came to his home and arrested him.

Sufian Belhaj Put the Truth About Tunisia on Facebook

"But now I have no reason to hide—they know who I am," he says, adding, "I was not tortured" during the three days in detention. "Actually, I was treated quite well. I guess they understood that their show was almost over."

He was released Sunday, the day after President Zine El Abidine Ben Ali fled to Saudi Arabia.

Belhaj is 28. He studied political science in Brussels, and returned to Tunisia a year ago. Like many other educated middle-class members of his generation, he was unable to find work. He spends much of his time on Facebook, Twitter and other social networks. Two months ago, he says, when WikiLeaks published the U.S. State Department documents, "I decided to translate into Arabic and French the documents about Tunisia. Of course, the citizens of Tunisia already knew these things, but this made it official."

American diplomats had gone into great detail and used colorful language to describe the "quasi-mafia" created by Ben Ali and the relatives of his wife, Leila Trabelsi.

"Whether it's cash, services, land, property—or, yes, even your yacht—President Ben Ali's family is rumored to covet it and reportedly gets what it wants," an American diplomat informed Washington.

Belhaj translated it all. "I knew the media here, which is under government control, would not publish it in any form, nor would the Arab press. Facebook was the way to sidestep censorship."

"WikiLeaks, Twitter and Facebook were the fuel for the revolution."

He posted the translations on a Facebook page via an account he opened under the name Hamadi Kaloutcha. Within a week he had 170,000 readers. It took the authorities a month to delete the page, but by then hundreds of bloggers and Internet users in Tunisia, along with Tunisians living abroad and people from other Arab countries, had copied and reposted the translations.

"It gave frustrated people information that appeared to be reliable, in place of the whispered rumors," Belhaj explains.

He doesn't know if Mohamed Bouazizi—the 26-year-old university graduate who immolated himself to protest the police's refusal to allow him even to sell vegetables in the market, and whose death triggered the national uprising—had read his translation.

"WikiLeaks, Twitter and Facebook were the fuel for the revolution," he says. "Bouazizi was the spark that ignited it all."

"After they arrested him without telling me where they were taking him," says Belhaj's wife, Ayish, who is 25, "I went on Facebook and recruited people to spread his story. The authorities could not ignore that."

Belhaj knows that Tunisia is still far from the democracy the thousands of demonstrators are demanding, but he feels he is part of a historic process: "Until now Tunisians had one historic date, 1956, when we received independence and Habib Bourguiba established the state. Now we have a new date—2011."

The Internet Was the Only Credible Source of Information

An estimated more than 20 percent of Tunisia's inhabitants use Facebook. Fatma Marwadi-Sudi, 53, a French teacher at a Tunis high school, says, "Since the demonstrations started I have been on the computer a few hours every day, looking for material, blogs, announcements and video clips from demonstrations, and I have forwarded them to others."

Tunisians do not trust the media, which is controlled by the ruling Constitutional Democratic Rally Party. "Television here did not show the demonstrations," Marwadi-Sudi says. "Everything we knew we got online. Our inspiration came from the demonstrations last year in Iran after the elections there."

She adds, "It's hard for me to interest the students in this, because they are used to the situation. One reason I learned to use the Internet was to interest them in what is happening around us. We also did a few more things on Twitter and Facebook: We published names of activists who were arrested and we provided the phone numbers of human rights organizations, lawyers and physicians who were ready to help."

For years there was a dissonance in Tunisia between the near-total political repression, achieved largely through the government's full control of the media, and the everyday life of a very secular society with full equality for women, a high level of education, a higher standard of living than other African countries and close ties with Western countries, particularly France.

"I was allowed to teach the French Revolution and talk about democracy and freedom," Marwadi-Sudi notes, "but I was prohibited from saying anything about what was happening here in the country."

Social Media Fail to Incite True Activism

Malcolm Gladwell

Malcolm Gladwell, named by Time *magazine in 2005 as one of the world's one hundred most influential people, is a staff writer for the* New Yorker *and the author of four books including* The Tipping Point: How Little Things Can Make a Big Difference *and* Blink: The Power of Thinking Without Thinking.

At four-thirty in the afternoon on Monday, February 1, 1960, four college students sat down at the lunch counter at the Woolworth's in downtown Greensboro, North Carolina. They were freshmen at North Carolina A&T, a black college a mile or so away.

"I'd like a cup of coffee, please," one of the four, Ezell Blair, said to the waitress.

"We don't serve Negroes here," she replied.

The Woolworth's lunch counter was a long L-shaped bar that could seat sixty-six people, with a stand-up snack bar at one end. The seats were for whites. The snack bar was for blacks. Another employee, a black woman who worked at the steam table, approached the students and tried to warn them away. "You're acting stupid, ignorant!" she said. They didn't move. Around five-thirty, the front doors to the store were locked. The four still didn't move. Finally, they left by a side door. Outside, a small crowd had gathered, including a photographer from the Greensboro *Record*. "I'll be back tomorrow with A& T College," one of the students said.

By next morning, the protest had grown to twenty-seven men and four women, most from the same dormitory as the original four....

By the following Monday, sit-ins had spread to Winston-Salem, twenty-five miles away, and Durham, fifty miles away. The day after that, students at Fayetteville State Teachers College and at Johnson C. Smith College, in Charlotte, joined in, followed on Wednesday by students at St. Augustine's College and Shaw University, in Raleigh. On Thursday and Friday, the protest crossed state lines, surfacing in Hampton and Portsmouth, Virginia, in Rock Hill, South Carolina, and in Chattanooga, Tennessee. By the end of the month, there were sit-ins throughout the South, as far west as Texas. "I asked every student I met what the first day of the sit-downs had been like on his campus," the political theorist Michael Walzer wrote in *Dissent*. "The answer was always the same: 'It was like a fever. Everyone wanted to go.'" Some seventy thousand students eventually took part. Thousands were arrested and untold thousands more radicalized. These events in the early sixties became a civil rights war that engulfed the South for the rest of the decade—and it happened without e-mail, texting, Facebook, or Twitter.

Fifty years after one of the most extraordinary episodes of social upheaval in American history, we seem to have forgotten what activism is.

Commentators Have Exaggerated the Role of Social Media

The world, we are told, is in the midst of a revolution. The new tools of social media have reinvented social activism. With Facebook and Twitter and the like, the traditional relationship between political authority and popular will has been upended, making it easier for the powerless to collaborate, coordinate, and give voice to their concerns. When ten thousand protesters took to the streets in Moldova in the spring of 2009 to protest against their country's Communist government, the action was dubbed the Twitter revolution, because of the means by which the demonstrators had been brought together. A few months after that, when student protests rocked Tehran, the State Department took the unusual step of asking Twitter to suspend scheduled maintenance of its website, because the administration didn't want such a critical organizing tool out of service at the height of the demonstrations. "Without Twitter the people of Iran would not have felt empowered and confident to stand up for freedom and democracy," Mark Pfeifle, a former national-security adviser, later wrote, calling for Twitter to be nominated for the Nobel Peace Prize. Where activists were once defined by their causes, they are now defined by their tools. Facebook warriors go online to push for change. "You are the best hope for us all," James K. Glassman, a former senior State Department official, told a crowd of cyber activists at a recent conference sponsored by Facebook, AT&T, Howcast, MTV, and Google. Sites like Facebook, Glassman said, "give the U.S. a significant competitive advantage over terrorists. Some time ago, I said that Al Qaeda was 'eating our lunch on the Internet.' That is no longer the case. Al Qaeda is stuck in Web 1.0. The Internet is now about interactivity and conversation."

These are strong, and puzzling, claims. Why does it matter who is eating whose lunch on the Internet? Are people who log on to their Facebook page really the best hope for us all? As for Moldova's so-called Twitter Revolution, Evgeny Morozov, a scholar at Stanford who has been the most persistent of digital evangelism's critics, points out that Twitter had scant internal significance in Moldova, a country where very few Twitter accounts exist. Nor does it seem to have been a revolution, not least because the protests—as Anne Applebaum suggested in the *Washington Post*—may well have been a bit of stagecraft cooked up by the government. (In a country paranoid about Romanian revanchism, the protesters flew a Romanian flag over the Parliament building.) In the Iranian case, meanwhile, the people tweeting about the demonstrations were almost all in the West. "It is time to get Twitter's role in the events in Iran right," Golnaz Esfandiari wrote, this past summer, in *Foreign Policy*. "Simply put: There was no Twitter Revolution inside Iran." The cadre of prominent bloggers, like Andrew Sullivan, who championed the role of social media in Iran, Esfandiari continued, misunderstood the situation. "Western journalists who couldn't reach—or didn't bother reaching?—people on the ground in Iran simply scrolled through the English-language tweets post with tag #iranelection," she wrote. "Through it all, no one seemed to wonder why people trying to coordinate protests in Iran would be writing in any language other than Farsi."

Some of this grandiosity is to be expected. Innovators tend to be solipsists. They often want to cram every stray fact and experience into their new model. As the historian Robert Darnton has written, "The marvels of communication technology in the present have produced a false consciousness about the past—even a sense that communication has no history, or had nothing of importance to consider before the days of television and the Internet." But there is something else at work here, in the outsized enthusiasm for social media. Fifty years after one of the most extraordinary episodes of social upheaval in American history, we seem to have forgotten what activism is.

High-risk activism . . . is a "strong tie" phenomenon.

The Civil Rights Movement Involved High-Risk Activism

Greensboro in the early 1960s was the kind of place where racial insubordination was routinely met with violence. The four students who first sat down at the lunch counter were terrified. . . .

The dangers were even clearer in the Mississippi Freedom Summer Project of 1964, another of the sentinel campaigns of the civil rights movement. The Student Nonviolent Coordinating Committee recruited hundreds of Northern, largely white unpaid volunteers to run Freedom Schools, register black voters, and raise civil rights awareness in the Deep South. "No one should go *anywhere* alone, but certainly not in an automobile and certainly not at night," they were instructed. Within days of arriving in Mississippi, three volunteers—Michael Schwerner, James Chaney, and Andrew Goodman—were kidnapped and killed, and, during the rest of the summer, thirty-seven black churches were set on fire and dozens of safe houses were bombed; volunteers were beaten, shot at, arrested, and trailed by pickup trucks full of armed men. A quarter of those in the program dropped out. Activism that challenges the status quo—that attacks deeply rooted problems—is not for the faint of heart.

What makes people capable of this kind of activism? The Stanford sociologist Doug McAdam compared the Freedom Summer dropouts with the participants who stayed, and discovered that the key difference wasn't, as might be expected, ideological fervor. "*All* of the applicants—participants and withdrawals alike—emerge as highly committed, articulate supporters of the goals and values of the summer program," he concluded. What mattered more was an applicant's degree of personal connection to the civil rights movement. All the volunteers were required to provide a list of personal contacts—the people they wanted kept apprised of their activities—and participants were far more likely than dropouts to have close friends who were also going to Mississippi. High-risk activism, McAdam concluded, is a "strong-tie" phenomenon. . . .

Social Media Is Built around Weak Ties

The kind of activism associated with social media isn't like this at all. The platforms of social media are built around weak ties. Twitter is a way of following (or being followed by) people you may never have met. Facebook is a tool for efficiently managing your acquaintances, for keeping up with the people you would not otherwise be able to stay in touch with. That's why you can have a thousand "friends" on Facebook, as you never could in real life.

This is in many ways a wonderful thing. There is strength in weak ties, as the sociologist Mark Granovetter has observed. Our acquaintances—not our friends—are our greatest source of new ideas and information. The Internet lets us exploit the power of these kinds of distant connections with marvelous efficiency. It's terrific at the diffusion of innovation, interdisciplinary collaboration, seamlessly matching up buyers and sellers, and the logistical functions of the dating world. But weak ties seldom lead to high-risk activism.

Social networks are effective at increasing participation—*by lessening the level of motivation that participation requires.*

In a new book called *The Dragonfly Effect: Quick, Effective, and Powerful Ways to Use Social Media to Drive Social Change*, the business consultant Andy Smith and the Stanford Business School professor Jennifer Aaker tell the story of Sameer Bhatia, a young Silicon Valley entrepreneur who came down with acute myelogenous leukemia. It's a perfect illustration of social media's strengths. Bhatia needed a bone-marrow transplant, but he could not find a match among his relatives and friends. The odds were best with a donor of his ethnicity, and there were few South Asians in the national bone-marrow database. So Bhatia's business partner sent out an e-mail explaining Bhatia's plight to more than four hundred of their acquaintances, who forwarded the e-mail to their personal contacts; Facebook pages and YouTube videos were devoted to the Help

Sameer campaign. Eventually, nearly twenty-five thousand new people were registered in the bone-marrow database, and Bhatia found a match.

But how did the campaign get so many people to sign up? By not asking too much of them. That's the only way you can get someone you don't really know to do something on your behalf. You can get thousands of people to sign up for a donor registry, because doing so is pretty easy. You have to send in a cheek swab and—in the highly unlikely event that your bone marrow is a good match for someone in need—spend a few hours at the hospital. Donating bone marrow isn't a trivial matter. But it doesn't involve financial or personal risk; it doesn't mean spending a summer being chased by armed men in pickup trucks. It doesn't require that you confront socially entrenched norms and practices. In fact, it's the kind of commitment that will bring only social acknowledgment and praise.

The evangelists of social media don't understand this distinction; they seem to believe that a Facebook friend is the same as a real friend and that signing up for a donor registry in Silicon Valley today is activism in the same sense as sitting at a segregated lunch counter in Greensboro in 1960. "Social networks are particularly effective at increasing motivation," Aaker and Smith write. But that's not true. Social networks are effective at increasing *participation*—by lessening the level of motivation that participation requires. . . . Facebook activism succeeds not by motivating people to make a real sacrifice but by motivating them to do the things that people do when they are not motivated enough to make a real sacrifice. We are a long way from the lunch counters of Greensboro.

The Civil Rights Movement Was Highly Organized

The students who joined the sit-ins across the South during the winter of 1960 described the movement as a "fever." But the civil rights movement was more like a military campaign than like a contagion. In the late 1950s, there had been sixteen sit-ins in various cities throughout the South, fifteen of which were formally organized by civil rights organizations like the NAACP [National Association for the Advancement of Colored People] and CORE. Possible locations for activism were scouted. Plans were drawn up. Movement activists held training sessions and retreats for would-be protesters. The Greensboro Four were a product of this groundwork: all were members of the NAACP Youth Council. They had close ties with the head of the local NAACP chapter. They had been briefed on the earlier wave of sit-ins in Durham, and had been part of a series of movement meetings in activist churches. When the sit-in movement spread from Greensboro throughout the South, it did not spread indiscriminately. It spread to those cities which had preexisting "movement centers"—a core of dedicated and trained activists ready to turn the "fever" into action.

Because networks don't have a centralized leadership structure and clear lines of authority, they have real difficulty reaching consensus and setting goals.

The civil rights movement was high-risk activism. It was also, crucially, strategic activism: a challenge to the establishment mounted with precision and discipline. The NAACP was a centralized organization, run from New York according to highly formalized operating procedures. At the Southern Christian Leadership Conference, Martin Luther King Jr. was the unquestioned authority. At the center of the movement was the black church, which had, as Aldon D. Morris points out in his superb 1984 study, *The Origins of the Civil Rights Movement*, a carefully demarcated division of labor, with various standing committees and disciplined groups. "Each group was task-oriented and coordinated its activities through authority structures," Morris writes. "Individuals were held accountable for their assigned duties, and important conflicts were resolved by the minister, who usually exercised ultimate authority over the congregation."

Social Networks Are Leaderless

This is the second crucial distinction between traditional activism and its online variant: Social media are not about this kind of hierarchical organization. Facebook and the like are tools for building *networks*, which are the opposite, in structure and character, of hierarchies. Unlike hierarchies, with their rules and procedures, networks aren't controlled by a single central authority. Decisions are made through consensus, and the ties that bind people to the group are loose.

This structure makes networks enormously resilient and adaptable in low-risk situations. Wikipedia is a perfect example. It doesn't have an editor, sitting in New York, who directs and corrects each entry. The effort of putting together each entry is self-organized. If every entry in Wikipedia were to be erased tomorrow, the content would swiftly be restored, because that's what happens when a network of thousands spontaneously devote their time to a task.

There are many things, though, that networks don't do well. Car companies sensibly use a network to organize their hundreds of suppliers, but not to design their cars. No one believes that the articulation of a coherent design philosophy is best handled by a sprawling, leaderless organizational system. Because networks don't have a centralized leadership structure and clear lines of authority, they have real difficulty reaching consensus and setting goals. They can't think strategically; they are chronically prone to conflict and error. How do you make difficult choices about tactics or strategy or philosophical direction when everyone has an equal say? . . .

The drawbacks of networks scarcely matter if the network isn't interested in systemic change—if it just wants to frighten or humiliate or make a splash—or if it doesn't need to think strategically. But if you're taking on a powerful and organized establishment you have to be a hierarchy. The Montgomery bus boycott required the participation of tens of thousands of people who depended on public transit to get to and from work each day. It lasted a *year*. In order to persuade those people to stay true to the cause, the boycott's organizers tasked each local black church with maintaining morale, and put together a free alternative private carpool service, with forty-eight dispatchers and forty-two pickup stations. Even the White Citizens' Council, King later said, conceded that the carpool system moved with "military precision." By the time King came to Birmingham, for the climactic showdown with Police Commissioner Eugene (Bull) Connor, he had a budget of a million dollars, and a hundred full-time staff members on the ground, divided into operational units. The operation itself was divided into steadily escalating phases, mapped out in advance. Support was maintained through consecutive mass meetings rotating from church to church around the city.

Boycotts and sit-ins and nonviolent confrontations—which were the weapons of choice for the civil rights movement—are high-risk strategies. They leave little room for conflict and error. The moment even one protester deviates from the script and responds to provocation, the moral legitimacy of the entire protest is compromised. Enthusiasts for social media would no doubt have us believe that King's task in Birmingham would have been made infinitely easier had he been able to communicate with his followers through Facebook, and contented himself with tweets from a Birmingham jail. But networks are messy: think of the ceaseless pattern of correction and revision, amendment and debate, that characterizes Wikipedia. If Martin Luther King Jr., had tried to do a wiki-boycott in Montgomery, he would have been steamrollered by the white power structure. And of what use would a digital communication tool be in a town where 98 percent of the black community could be reached every Sunday morning at church? The things that King needed in Birmingham—discipline and strategy—were things that online social media cannot provide.

The Role of Social Media in Iran Was Exaggerated

Evgeny Morozov

Evgeny Morozov is a contributing editor and blogger for Foreign Policy *and the author of* The Net Delusion: The Dark Side of Internet Freedom. *He is a visiting scholar at Stanford University and a Schwartz fellow at the New America Foundation.*

Among the unpleasant surprises that awaited Barack Obama's administration during the post-election turmoil in Iran, the unexpected role of the Internet must have been most rankling. A few government wonks might have expected Iranians to rebel, but who could predict they would do so using Silicon Valley's favorite toys? Team Obama, never shy to tout its mastery of all things digital, was caught off guard and, at least for a moment or two, appeared ill-informed about the heady developments in Iranian cyberspace.

Speaking a few days after the protests began, Secretary of State Hillary Clinton confessed that she wouldn't know "a Twitter from a tweeter, but apparently, it's very important"— referring to Twitter, a popular mix between a blogging service and a social network that enables its users to exchange brief messages of up to 140 characters in length.

Western Media Overstated the Role of Twitter

While Clinton's response must have pacified aging American diplomats, uneasy about the prospect of attending new-media workshops to bolster their Internet expertise, it didn't really comport with the popular narrative of events unfolding in Tehran, at least not the one constructed by the U.S. media. This

Evgeny Morozov, "Iran: Downside to the 'Twitter Revolution,'" *Dissent*, v. 56, no. 4, Fall 2009, pp. 10–14. Copyright © 2010 by the University of Pennsylvania Press. All rights reserved. Reproduced by permission of the University of Pennsylvania Press.

narrative had come to be known as "Iran's Twitter Revolution." In the first days after the protests, it was hard to find a television network or a newspaper (never mind the blogs) that didn't run a feature or an editorial extolling the role of Twitter in fomenting and publicizing the Iranian protests. The modish take of the usually sober *Christian Science Monitor* is representative of the heavily skewed coverage: "The government's tight control of the Internet has spawned a generation adept at circumventing cyber roadblocks, making the country ripe for a technology-driven protest movement."

Whether technology was actually driving the protests remains a big unknown. It is certainly a theory that many in the West find endearing: Who would have expected that after decades of blasting propaganda from dedicated radio and television channels, Americans would be able to support democracy in Iran via blogs and social networks? Nice theory, but it has very little basis in reality; in fact, it is mostly American rather than Iranian bloggers who are culpable for blowing the role of technology out of any reasonable proportion. Andrew Sullivan, who was tirelessly blogging about the events in Tehran for the *Atlantic*, emerged as one of the few comprehensive one-stop shops for real-time updates from Iran (or, to be more precise, from the Iranian Internet). Sullivan (and the *Huffington Post*'s Nico Pitney) made a significant contribution to how the rest of the media—cut off from access to the streets of Tehran and unable to navigate the new-media maze as effectively as well-trained bloggers portrayed the protests. It was Sullivan who famously proclaimed "The Revolution Will Be Twittered" and called Twitter "the critical tool for organizing the resistance in Iran." If Iran's Twitter Revolution needs a godfather, Andrew Sullivan has the best credentials in town.

It is easy to see why so many pundits accepted this narrative: They had seen something similar before. The exultant hordes of attractive, obstreperous young people, armed with fax machines and an occasional Xerox copier, taking on the brutal dictators—and winning: that already happened twenty years ago, and the venue was Eastern Europe. The parallels with Iran were too striking to resist. "Tehran's 'collective action cascade' of 2009 feels like Leipzig [Germany] 1989," tweeted Clay Shirky, new media's favorite cheerleader, who is always au courant with latest trends. In an interview with TED.com, Shirky claimed that "[Iran's] is the first revolution that has been catapulted onto a global stage and transformed by social media." However, as [Iranian president] Mahmoud Ahmadinejad and [Iranian spiritual leader] Ayatollah Ali Khamenei, who were, perhaps, even more surprised by the high-tech protests than Obama, began their ruthless crackdown, the hopes of another "velvet revolution" quickly faded away, and virtually all pundits, including Sullivan, cured themselves of their Twitter obsession almost as rapidly as they had developed it. Tehran, caught up now in a bloodcurdling Stalinist [referring to the Soviet Union premier Joseph Stalin] show trial had successfully deflected the Twitter threat, and the revolutionary spirit had been whittled down. What seemed like Leipzig in 1989 was beginning to resemble Beijing of the same year.

This new media ecosystem is very much like the old game of "Telephone," in which errors steadily accumulate in the transmission process.

The Western Media Relied on Pro-West Bloggers for Information

So, what to make of Iran's Twitter Revolution? Has it upended any of our assumptions about the political power of the Internet? Plenty of skeptics think it was just a myth, dreamed up and advanced by cyber-utopian Western commentators, who finally got a chance to prove that the billions of hours that humanity wastes on Twitter and Facebook are not spent in vain. Critics counter that the failure of the Twitter Revolution doesn't mean that new media didn't play an important role in it. By bashing Twitter, we are blinding ourselves to the looming age of cheap and effective Internet-powered protests that will soon extirpate all forms of authoritarianism.

On first examination, the former charge has some merit. It is, indeed, quite easy to dismiss the Twitter Revolution as a product of the wild imagination—or, perhaps, the excessive optimism—of our self-anointed Internet gurus and visionaries. Many of them do offer superb analysis of technology's role in national affairs. But they invariably flounder when it comes to analyzing technology's role in global politics, offering a very parochial and superficial analysis of the situation. This is one subject area where they are severely inhibited by their lack of familiarity with foreign Internet cultures. Knowing something about local politics is not enough to understand the role that the Internet plays in a given context. Moreover, they often can't read the language and have limited information to work with.

Of course, they can still guess the nature and direction of the local conversations; their "cheat sheet" consists of following bilingual bloggers, who write in both their native language and English, and subscribing to blog aggregators like Global Voices, which purport to aggregate interesting conversations happening in non-English environments. The most curious and demanding could also use various machine translation tools that translate blogs from, say, Farsi to English. Some laud the emergence of this new media ecosystem: at what other point in history did we have a chance to tap directly into the thought process of young Iranians? It was the dwindling tribe of foreign correspondents that used to find those people for us and make them leading characters of their periodic, offbeat "Letter from . . ." dispatches. Today, the argument goes, we should thank Twitter for allowing us to follow them on a daily basis and in real time and—here is the punch line—to follow all of them, finally unshackling ourselves from the inherent biases of cigar-smoking and Martini-sipping white men.

By its very design Twitter only adds to the noise: It's simply impossible to pack much context into its 140 characters.

In reality, however, this new media ecosystem is very much like the old game of "Telephone," in which errors steadily accumulate in the transmission process, and the final message has nothing in common with the original. Judging by the flawed media coverage of the events in Tehran, the game never sounded more Iranian. Thus, to blame Andrew Sullivan for first dreaming up the "Twitter Revolution," we have to blame a bevy of English-speaking Iranian bloggers who had shaped his opinion (many of them from the Iranian diaspora, with strong pro-Western feelings—why else blog in English?), as well as Farsi-speaking bloggers in Tehran who had shaped the opinion of the English-speaking Iranians, and so forth. Factor in various political biases, and it becomes clear that what Andrew Sullivan is "seeing" might be radically different from what is actually happening.

The traditional media, banned from reporting from Tehran (and, in many cases, unable to finance their stay there anyway), have to feed off the bloggers rather than do their own reporting or sift through thousands of often apocryphal posts from unknown writers. This only amplifies the noise. Thus, it's hardly surprising that we are prone to see trends and developments that only exist in the minds of our local interlocutors. Learning from foreign blogs is a long and tedious process; it is largely useless in times of a crisis—who has time to read and translate blog posts when people are dying in the streets?—so it's quite logical that Twitter, with its 140-character limit and its cult of immediacy, has emerged as a key source of news and updates from Tehran. It is, indeed, a great short-cut to viewing the photos, videos, or text updates from the Iranian streets that resurface on our favorite blogs a few hours later.

Only a Small Number of Iranians Use Twitter

However, by its very design Twitter only adds to the noise: It's simply impossible to pack much context into its 140 characters. Other biases are present as well: In a country like Iran it's mostly pro-Western, technology-friendly and iPod-carrying young people who are the natural and most frequent users of Twitter. They are a tiny and, most important, extremely untypical segment of the Iranian population (the number of Twitter users in Iran—a country of more than seventy million people—was estimated at less than twenty thousand before the protests). Whatever they do with Twitter may have little relevance to the rest of the country, including the masses marching in the streets. However, if these hip young people are our only way of getting information from the ground, it's quite natural that we also see them as "agents of change," who must be instrumental in organizing the protests. On a purely cognitive level, we are quick to make the connection between the fact that there are thousands of people marching or demonstrating in the streets and the fact that these young peoples' Twitter updates are read by thousands (most of whom live outside of Iran). But this connection is imaginary.

To ascribe such great importance to Twitter is to disregard the fact that it is very poorly suited to planning protests in a repressive environment like Iran's. The protests that engulfed the streets of Tehran were not spontaneous nor were they "flashmobs"; they were carefully planned and executed by the Moussavi camp. The "flashmob" scenario may have worked in Moldova—the previous host of a "Twitter revolution"—where a dozen young people had, indeed, transformed a flashmob into a massive rally earlier in the year. But Iran's protests were radically different; unlike Moldova, it had a well-organized opposition that was expecting the election to be rigged and was prepared to take action. That the Iranian opposition would venture into Twitter territory to deliberate about the best venue for its next march is ridiculous, not only because it seems pointless (after all, the Bolsheviks [extremists during the Russian Revolution in 1917] didn't have to use deliberative polling to choose the Winter Palace as their target) but because the Iranian secret services would probably read these deliberations before anyone else did—and then take preemptive action.

Authoritarian Regimes Are Using Social Media

A Twitter revolution is only possible in a regime where the state apparatus is completely ignorant of the Internet and has no virtual presence of its own. However, most authoritarian states are now moving in the opposite direction, eagerly exploiting cyberspace for their own strategic purposes. Even technology laggards like North Korea are increasingly accused of harboring cyberwarfare ambitions. As it happens, both Twitter and Facebook give Iran's secret services superb platforms for gathering open source intelligence about the future revolutionaries, revealing how they are connected to each other. These details are now being shared voluntarily, without any external pressure. Once regimes used torture to get this kind of data; now it's freely available on Facebook.

Unfortunately, such nuances are lost on young Iranians and their foreign supporters; they happily exchange public messages with each other, creating a very dangerous trail of evidence that, sooner or later, could be used against them—in the case of Iranians, probably sooner, in court. Imagine a possible question: "How do you explain that a dozen suspicious Americans contacted you on Twitter? Are you a spy?" Well, it's certainly not the first revolution (albeit only a Twitter one) where well-meaning but extremely naive foreigners may have harmed their favorite causes. However, in the past one needed a fortune or, at least, a good name to cause much damage. Today all one needs is an Internet connection.

Understanding how the Internet fits a particular political and social environment is one of the most intellectually challenging tasks facing the U.S. foreign policy apparatus.

For example, realizing that one way to help the protesters is to clog the Iranian propaganda machine, some enthusiastic American Twitterati began sharing tips on how to attack the key news websites of the Iranian government. Their campaign quickly went viral. After all, what could be more exciting than the prospect of attacking the evil government of Ahmadinejad from the comfort of one's favorite café? Cyber-solidarity has never felt so good. What these cyber-soldiers didn't expect was that their attacks would also slow down the entire Iranian Internet, making it difficult to obtain any (even nongovernment) information or upload photos or videos from the protests. Thus, foreign supporters of the Twitter Revolution managed to do what the Iranian government couldn't: make the Internet unusable for activists. Another disturbing group that suddenly got its fair share of action in cyberspace were citizen vigilantes; blogs and Twitter accounts that looked "suspicious"—that is, appeared to be spreading "misinformation" about the venues and times of the protests as well as the reaction from authorities—were publicly named and shamed on dedicated sites (Twitterspam.com was one such site). Getting off the lists was not easy; the Twitterati didn't have much tolerance or appetite for dissent.

This dark side of the "Twitter Revolution" didn't get much play in the media; nevertheless, it illustrates how poorly planned online activism can backfire. But harmless activism wasn't very productive either: What do 100 million people invited to join the Facebook group "100 Million Facebook members for Democracy in Iran" expect to get out of their membership? Is it just a gigantic exercise in collective transcontinental wishful thinking? Do they really expect that their "slacktivism"—a catchy new word that describes such feelgood but useless Internet activism—would have some impact? Slacktivists may successfully grapple with corporate PR [public relations] outfits that have increasingly grown fond of polluting and astroturfing cyberspace; whether they will be able to topple authoritarian governments is less obvious.

There Are Lessons for the US Government

While Iran's "Twitter Revolution" has proven to be a damp squib, members of the Obama administration have much to learn from it. Before they get carried away with their immutable cyber-utopianism, they'd better study the role that the Internet didn't play as well as the reasons for it. Understanding how the Internet fits a particular political and social environment is one of the most intellectually challenging tasks facing the U.S. foreign policy apparatus in the next decade. So far, its members haven't even scratched the surface; what's worse, the Utopian tech-enthusiasts who advise them are constantly steering the ship in the wrong direction. However, there might also be a silver lining to having the U.S. media overstate the case for the Twitter Revolution: Thousands of Iranian young people may now want to experiment with Twitter and see what it has to offer. It's important that the old guard of American public diplomacy—entities like the Broadcasting Board of Governors—be fully prepared to satisfy these demands, embracing Twitter as a useful tool of generating and spreading views critical of regimes like Ahmadinejad's.

Above all, the U.S. government needs to be prepared to radically rethink the role of Cold War–era institutions like the

Voice of America and Radio Free Europe and deal with the fact that they may soon be less effective than the more nimble and popular platforms like Twitter and Facebook. Thus, it's not only its relations with key American nemeses that the Obama administration needs to reset; it's also how it thinks about the web. Learning how to distinguish a "Twitter from a tweeter" would be a good first step; getting realistic about what the Internet can and cannot do would be a good second one.

Social Media Did Not Cause the Egyptian Revolution

Parvez Sharma

Parvez Sharma is a New York–based Indian writer and film-maker best known for the film A Jihad for Love.

Cairo is burning. So is Egypt. Twitter is exploding. Every-one seems to have an opinion—many who have never even been to Egypt, but feel a strong sense of solidarity with the most remarkable revolution in a generation, perhaps. A revolution that importantly is not really caused by Twitter or by Facebook—as much as the self-congratulatory social net-working types in the West would like to believe.

Most Commentators Are Clueless About Egypt

Full disclosure: Sleepless but still sitting in relative comfort in my Manhattan apartment I am one of those relentless tweet-ers. However my obsession stems from a long love and asso-ciation with Egypt and the presence of way too many friends who have jumped into the chaos not really knowing what consequences their actions might have for themselves or their friends and families.

I must also be clear. At this point—on this, the longest Egyptian night in a generation, perhaps longer—most Western self-professed Islam/Middle East and other assorted pundits have no clue about the harsh reality of Egyptian life. Many have probably never taken a walk down Manshiyat Naser, the largest slum in Cairo. This is why they do not realize that this "revolution" is not about social networking and its success. The majority of the 80 million people of Egypt live in abject poverty. They do not even have cell phones let alone smart-phones like the iPhone or the Droid. They go to kiosks to make calls. A pretty substantial number of them have NEVER used the Internet and do not have email accounts: The complicated mechanisms of self-promotion and information gathering and sharing on social networks is not a part of their lives—they have never had the money or the resources to get access to this other world that often lives in the relatively more affluent neighborhoods like Zamalek or Garden City or Mohandeseen—all within some walking distance of where the dissent started in Tahrir Square.

Most Protesters Aren't Using Social Networks

The majority of the protesters in Cairo, in Suez, in Alexandria, in Luxor, in Mahla, in Mansoura, and all over this ancient land that is the very heart of what it means to be Arab, are not "twittering" or "Facebooking" or "emailing" or even watching the landmark live coverage that Al Jazeera is providing. They are out on the streets—and yes, without phone access—risking their lives and giving vent to three decades, and perhaps more, of anger.

They are fighting for very basic human rights. They are fighting for affordable food. They are fighting for dignity. They are fighting for accountability. They are fighting to somehow improve the nonexistent financial opportunities in their lives.

They are not interested in Mohamed ElBaradei's Nobel Prize or his rather recent and opportunist political ambitions. Most of them have not really seen him and have no idea of what he has been up to for the last three decades as they have suffered. They are angry that he decided to show up just last night and started posturing immediately as the potential savior and the best person to lead them into their uncertain future. Many here in the West would be surprised to know that a lot of these simple folk would actually prefer the "Muslim Brotherhood" taking over. At least they recognize the "Islam Light" the Brotherhood has honed to perfection after a pretty radical and conservative beginning with an ideologue like Hasan al-Banna.

CHAPTER 4

Should People Have Unrestricted Access to Social Networks?

Overview: Technology Makes It Harder for Repressive Governments to Censor

William J. Dobson

William J. Dobson is a visiting scholar at the Carnegie Endowment for International Peace and a frequent contributor to many publications, including the New York Times *and* Washington Post.

For Austin Heap, there was nothing particularly remarkable about June 14, 2009. The 25-year-old computer programmer was home in his San Francisco apartment, spending his evening the same way he spent much of his free time: playing video games. "I was sitting at my computer, as I usually do, playing Warcraft," recalls Heap. "My boyfriend asked if I was following what was going on in Iran, and I said no. I was busy killing dragons."

Later that night, Heap logged on to his Twitter account. He read about the growing number of Iranians claiming that their votes had been stolen in the presidential election, and he saw people complaining that the government was censoring their cries of fraud and election rigging. For Heap—who says, "I am for human rights, the Internet, and I check out from there"—something clicked. At that moment, he decided to become involved in a battle more than 7,000 miles away in a country he admits he knew next to nothing about. "I remember literally saying, 'OK, game on.'"

Since the Internet came into its own, there has been no shortage of breathless expectation about what technology would do for the world's least-free places. Put simply, democratizing technologies were supposed to lead to democracy.

They didn't. Only later did people realize that the technology was just a tool; what mattered was how it was used. And authoritarian regimes initially proved to be more sophisticated than their opponents at wielding these new weapons.

"Four days ago I was killing dragons with my firepower ... and now I was getting leaks from inside the Iranian government."

Hackers Are Fighting Censorship

Now a new generation of hacktivists like Heap is fighting back. They are not seeking silver-bullet solutions but scalable technologies that will unlock the one advantage the people always had—the sheer power of their numbers. "The technology variable doesn't matter the most," says Patrick Meier, director of crisis mapping for Ushahidi, a group of digital activists doing cutting-edge work in open-source interactive mapping. "It is the organizational structure that will matter the most. Rigid structures are unable to adapt as quickly to a rapidly changing environment as a decentralized system. Ultimately, it is a battle of organizational theory."

That's one of the first lessons Heap learned when he took on the Iranians. In many authoritarian countries with a closely monitored Internet, citizens evade the state by using proxy servers that mask their identity as they surf the web. So, at first, Heap thought it would be helpful to create safe proxies that people in Iran could use. He posted advice on his blog about how people could run proxies from home. He soon had nearly 10,000 people following his instructions. But his efforts were almost pointless; Heap was taking on the Islamic Republic in a game of one on one, and he was no match. The regime's censors apparently read his blog, too, and simply trailed behind him, closing proxies as he pronounced them ready to use. "We could watch Iran respond," says Heap. "We would do something, and they would block it."

But then he had a stroke of luck. Someone with the online handle Quotemstr asked Heap to join a specific chatroom. Quotemstr wasn't interested in making idle conversation. He was a disaffected Iranian official with information to share. He provided Heap with a copy of the internal operating procedures for Iran's filtering software. The 96-page document was in Farsi, but the diagrams told Heap what he needed to know. (A computer savant, Heap learned his first programming language in fourth grade; he was programming in 18 languages by his senior year in high school.) "Four days ago I was killing dragons with my firepower," he recalls, "and now I was getting leaks from inside the Iranian government."

A Hacker Gets the US Government to Help

Less than a month and many all-nighters later, Heap and a friend had created Haystack. The anti-censorship software is built on a sophisticated mathematical formula that conceals someone's real online destinations inside a stream of innocuous traffic. You may be browsing an opposition website, but to the censors it will appear you are visiting, say, weather.com. Heap tends to hide users in content that is popular in Tehran, sometimes the regime's own government mouthpieces. Haystack is a step forward for activists working in repressive environments. Other anti-censorship programs—such as Tor, Psiphon, or Freegate—can successfully hide someone's identity, but censors are able to detect that these programs are being run and then work to disable the communication. With Haystack, the censors aren't even aware the software is in use. "Haystack captures all outgoing connections, encrypts them, and then masquerades the data as something else," explains Heap. "If you want to block Haystack, you are gonna block yourself."

The biggest hurdle Heap had to clear was, surprisingly, his own government. Because of the United States' strict sanctions laws barring trade with Iran, it was actually illegal for Heap to distribute a software program in Iran, even if it was aimed at promoting freedom. But his innovation caught the attention of the State Department, and it was fast-tracked for speedy approval. In the past year, he has also cofounded the Censorship Research Center, a nonprofit dedicated to fighting censorship everywhere. When I first met Heap in January [2010], he was regularly shuttling to Washington, D.C., for meetings at State and Treasury and with senior lawmakers. "Tomorrow I meet with [Sens. John] McCain, [Bob] Casey, maybe [Carl] Levin, but I don't know if I will have enough time," he told me, wearing jeans and a well-worn T shirt that said SUPER CHEVROLET SERVICE.

The only way to stay ahead in this cyberwar, though, is to play offense, not defense.

With his U.S. government waivers in hand, Heap is now deploying Haystack in Iran. His one-word mantra is "scalable." Heap intends to gradually develop Haystack's presence in the country. He has started to share it with select activists and trusted individuals on an invitation-only basis. They will then be asked to share it with their friends. It is the same model that was originally followed by Google's Gmail. The targeted approach is smarter from a security standpoint. Also, he doesn't want the software to collapse from low-value demand. "It is better to focus on people who are active than people pirating music," says Heap. "Organic growth is going to be much more successful than trying to blanket the country."

Hackers Have a Hit List of Authoritarian Countries

Of course, Iran will use any method—sophisticated or not—to counter such efforts. The Iranian regime has long made its presence felt online, blocking sites or redirecting traffic to government-run websites. Tehran frequently throttles the country's bandwidth, especially when protests are planned, to make uploading video or images painfully slow, if not impossible. And, just as the Revolutionary Guards have taken a greater role in most areas of the country's political, social, and economic life, so too have they become the dominant force policing Iran's virtual world. In May, a senior member of the Revolutionary Guards bragged that the regime has built the world's second-largest cyberarmy, after China's. Created last year and known as the Cyber Defense Command, this unit is believed to be behind most of the hacking and infiltration of opposition websites and e-mail accounts. Heap says it would be naive to think the regime won't target Haystack, and he claims to have thought through not only the countermeasures "one, two, and three . . . but also four, five, and six."

The only way to stay ahead in this cyberwar, though, is to play offense, not defense. "If it is a cat-and-mouse game," says Meier of Ushahidi, "by definition, the cat will adopt the mouse's technology, and vice versa." His view is that activists will have to get better at adopting some of the same tactics states use. Just as authoritarian governments try to block Voice of America broadcasts, so protest movements could use newer technology to jam state propaganda on radio or TV. In Iran, activists are experimenting with ways to use new tech tools to cripple the government's surveillance cameras, effectively blinding its eyes in the sky. The hacktivists will also have to reappraise their technology constantly, to see how else it might be used. Meier's own organization began as a web platform to map violence erupting in Kenya after that country's elections in 2007. As a tool, Ushahidi—which means "testimony" in Swahili—works in near real time to create crisis maps by integrating reports from people on the ground via e-mail, text, or the web. The technology proved critical in shaping the disaster response to the earthquakes in Haiti and Chile and is credited with saving hundreds of lives. Although Ushahidi is best known today for aiding humanitarian missions, opposition groups are now using this scalable open-source technology to expose election tampering or voter intimidation in places like Burma and Sudan. It has also been downloaded in Iran.

The gradual, go-slow approach of Heap and others shouldn't mask their ambition. After such an extraordinary year, I asked him where he hoped his organization would be a year from now. "I hope we are ready to take on the next country," he replied. "We will systematically take on each repressive country that censors its people. We have a list. Don't piss off hackers who will have their way with you. A mischievous kid will show you how the Internet works." The world's dictators should consider themselves on notice.

Internet Freedom Is an Essential Global Freedom

Hillary Rodham Clinton

Hillary Rodham Clinton is the US secretary of state during the Barack Obama administration and has served as US senator from New York.

The spread of information networks is forming a new nervous system for our planet. When something happens in Haiti or Hunan [a province of China], the rest of us learn about it in real time—from real people. And we can respond in real time as well. Americans eager to help in the aftermath of a disaster . . . are connected in ways that were not even imagined a year ago, even a generation ago. That same principle applies to almost all of humanity today. As we sit here, any of you—or maybe more likely, any of our children—can take out the tools that many carry every day and transmit this discussion to billions across the world.

The US Believes the Internet Should Be Free

Now, in many respects, information has never been so free. There are more ways to spread more ideas to more people than at any moment in history. And even in authoritarian countries, information networks are helping people discover new facts and making governments more accountable.

During his visit to China in November [2009], for example, President [Barack] Obama held a town hall meeting with an online component to highlight the importance of the Internet. In response to a question that was sent in over the Internet, he defended the right of people to freely access infor-

Secretary of State Hillary Rodham Clinton, "Remarks on Internet Freedom," January 21, 2010. www.state.gov.

mation, and said that the more freely information flows, the stronger societies become. He spoke about how access to information helps citizens hold their own governments accountable, generates new ideas, and encourages creativity and entrepreneurship. The United States' belief in that ground truth is what brings me here today.

We stand for a single Internet where all of humanity has equal access to knowledge and ideas.

Because amid this unprecedented surge in connectivity, we must also recognize that these technologies are not an unmitigated blessing. These tools are also being exploited to undermine human progress and political rights. Just as steel can be used to build hospitals or machine guns, or nuclear power can either energize a city or destroy it, modern information networks and the technologies they support can be harnessed for good or for ill. The same networks that help organize movements for freedom also enable al Qaeda to spew hatred and incite violence against the innocent. And technologies with the potential to open up access to government and promote transparency can also be hijacked by governments to crush dissent and deny human rights.

In the last year [2009], we've seen a spike in threats to the free flow of information. China, Tunisia, and Uzbekistan have stepped up their censorship of the Internet; in Vietnam, access to popular social networking sites has suddenly disappeared. And last Friday [January 15, 2010], in Egypt, 30 bloggers and activists were detained. One member of this group, Bassem Samir, who is thankfully no longer in prison, is with us today. So while it is clear that the spread of these technologies is transforming our world, it is still unclear how that transformation will affect the human rights and the human welfare of the world's population.

On their own, new technologies do not take sides in the struggle for freedom and progress, but the United States does. We stand for a single Internet where all of humanity has equal access to knowledge and ideas. And we recognize that the world's information infrastructure will become what we and others make of it. Now, this challenge may be new, but our responsibility to help ensure the free exchange of ideas goes back to the birth of our republic. The words of the First Amendment to our Constitution are carved in 50 tons of Tennessee marble on the front of this building. And every generation of Americans has worked to protect the values etched in that stone.

Internet Freedom Is a Human Right

Franklin Roosevelt built on these ideas when he delivered his Four Freedoms speech in 1941. Now, at the time, Americans faced a cavalcade of crises and a crisis of confidence. But the vision of a world in which all people enjoyed freedom of expression, freedom of worship, freedom from want, and freedom from fear transcended the troubles of his day. And years later, one of my heroes, Eleanor Roosevelt, worked to have these principles adopted as a cornerstone of the Universal Declaration of Human Rights. They have provided a lodestar to every succeeding generation, guiding us, galvanizing us, and enabling us to move forward in the face of uncertainty.

So as technology hurtles forward, we must think back to that legacy. We need to synchronize our technological progress with our principles. In accepting the Nobel Prize, President Obama spoke about the need to build a world in which peace rests on the inherent rights and dignities of every individual. And in my speech on human rights at Georgetown a few days later, I talked about how we must find ways to make human rights a reality. Today, we find an urgent need to protect these freedoms on the digital frontiers of the 21st century.

There are many other networks in the world. Some aid in the movement of people or resources, and some facilitate exchanges between individuals with the same work or interests. But the Internet is a network that magnifies the power and potential of all others. And that's why we believe it's critical that its users are assured certain basic freedoms. Freedom of expression is first among them. This freedom is no longer defined solely by whether citizens can go into the town square and criticize their government without fear of retribution. Blogs, e-mails, social networks, and text messages have opened up new forums for exchanging ideas, and created new targets for censorship.

Dictators Are Restricting the Free Flow of Information

As I speak to you today, government censors somewhere are working furiously to erase my words from the records of history. But history itself has already condemned these tactics. Two months ago [in November 2009], I was in Germany to celebrate the 20th anniversary of the fall of the Berlin Wall. The leaders gathered at that ceremony paid tribute to the courageous men and women on the far side of that barrier who made the case against oppression by circulating small pamphlets called samizdat. Now, these leaflets questioned the claims and intentions of dictatorships in the Eastern Bloc and many people paid dearly for distributing them. But their words helped pierce the concrete and concertina wire of the Iron Curtain.

The Berlin Wall symbolized a world divided and it defined an entire era. Today, remnants of that wall sit inside this museum where they belong, and the new iconic infrastructure of our age is the Internet. Instead of division, it stands for connection. But even as networks spread to nations around the globe, virtual walls are cropping up in place of visible walls.

Some countries have erected electronic barriers that prevent their people from accessing portions of the world's networks. They've expunged words, names, and phrases from search engine results. They have violated the privacy of citizens who engage in nonviolent political speech. These actions contravene the Universal Declaration of Human Rights, which tells us that all people have the right "to seek, receive and impart information and ideas through any media and regardless of frontiers." With the spread of these restrictive practices, a new information curtain is descending across much of the world. And beyond this partition, viral videos and blog posts are becoming the samizdat of our day.

As in the dictatorships of the past, governments are targeting independent thinkers who use these tools. In the demonstrations that followed Iran's presidential elections, grainy cell phone footage of a young woman's bloody murder provided a digital indictment of the government's brutality. We've seen reports that when Iranians living overseas posted online criticism of their nation's leaders, their family members in Iran were singled out for retribution. And despite an intense campaign of government intimidation, brave citizen journalists in Iran continue using technology to show the world and their fellow citizens what is happening inside their country. In speaking out on behalf of their own human rights, the Iranian people have inspired the world. And their courage is redefining how technology is used to spread truth and expose injustice.

Free Expression Has Limits

Now, all societies recognize that free expression has its limits. We do not tolerate those who incite others to violence, such as the agents of al Qaeda who are, at this moment, using the Internet to promote the mass murder of innocent people across the world. And hate speech that targets individuals on the basis of their race, religion, ethnicity, gender, or sexual orientation is reprehensible. It is an unfortunate fact that these issues are both growing challenges that the international community must confront together. And we must also grapple with the issue of anonymous speech. Those who use the Internet to recruit terrorists or distribute stolen intellectual property cannot divorce their online actions from their real-world identities. But these challenges must not become an excuse for governments to systematically violate the rights and privacy of those who use the Internet for peaceful political purposes.

The freedom of expression may be the most obvious freedom to face challenges with the spread of new technologies, but it is not the only one. The freedom of worship usually involves the rights of individuals to commune or not commune with their Creator. And that's one channel of communication that does not rely on technology. But the freedom of worship also speaks to the universal right to come together with those who share your values and vision for humanity. In our history, those gatherings often took place in churches, synagogues, mosques and temples. Today, they may also take place online.

The Internet can serve as a great equalizer. By providing people with access to knowledge and potential markets, networks can create opportunities where none exist.

The Internet can help bridge divides between people of different faiths. As the president said in Cairo, freedom of religion is central to the ability of people to live together. And as we look for ways to expand dialogue, the Internet holds out such tremendous promise. We've already begun connecting students in the United States with young people in Muslim communities around the world to discuss global challenges. And we will continue using this tool to foster discussion between individuals from different religious communities.

Some nations, however, have co-opted the Internet as a tool to target and silence people of faith. Last year, for example, in Saudi Arabia, a man spent months in prison for blogging about Christianity. And a Harvard study found that the Saudi government blocked many web pages about Hinduism, Judaism, Christianity, and even Islam. Countries including Vietnam and China employed similar tactics to restrict access to religious information.

Now, just as these technologies must not be used to punish peaceful political speech, they must also not be used to persecute or silence religious minorities. Now, prayers will always travel on higher networks. But connection technologies like the Internet and social networking sites should enhance individuals' ability to worship as they see fit, come together with people of their own faith, and learn more about the beliefs of others. We must work to advance the freedom of worship online just as we do in other areas of life.

The Internet Can Aid Economic Progress

There are, of course, hundreds of millions of people living without the benefits of these technologies. In our world, as I've said many times, talent may be distributed universally, but opportunity is not. And we know from long experience that promoting social and economic development in countries where people lack access to knowledge, markets, capital, and opportunity can be frustrating and sometimes futile work. In this context, the Internet can serve as a great equalizer. By providing people with access to knowledge and potential markets, networks can create opportunities where none exist.

Over the last year, I've seen this firsthand in Kenya, where farmers have seen their income grow by as much as 30 percent since they started using mobile banking technology; in Bangladesh, where more than 300,000 people have signed up to learn English on their mobile phones; and in sub-Saharan

Africa, where women entrepreneurs use the Internet to get access to microcredit loans and connect themselves to global markets.

As we work to advance freedoms, we must also work against those who use communication networks as tools of disruption and fear.

Now, these examples of progress can be replicated in the lives of the billion people at the bottom of the world's economic ladder. In many cases, the Internet, mobile phones, and other connection technologies can do for economic growth what the Green Revolution did for agriculture. You can now generate significant yields from very modest inputs. And one World Bank study found that in a typical developing country, a 10 percent increase in the penetration rate for mobile phones led to an almost 1 percent increase in per capita GDP [gross domestic product]. To just put this into context, for India, that would translate into almost $10 billion a year.

A connection to global information networks is like an on-ramp to modernity. In the early years of these technologies, many believed that they would divide the world between haves and have-nots. But that hasn't happened. There are 4 billion cell phones in use today. Many of them are in the hands of market vendors, rickshaw drivers, and others who've historically lacked access to education and opportunity. Information networks have become a great leveler, and we should use them together to help lift people out of poverty and give them a freedom from want.

Now, we have every reason to be hopeful about what people can accomplish when they leverage communication networks and connection technologies to achieve progress. But make no mistake—some are and will continue to use global information networks for darker purposes. Violent extremists, criminal cartels, sexual predators, and authoritarian governments all seek to exploit these global networks. Just as terrorists have taken advantage of the openness of our societies to carry out their plots, violent extremists use the Internet to radicalize and intimidate. As we work to advance freedoms, we must also work against those who use communication networks as tools of disruption and fear.

Those who disrupt the free flow of information in our society or any other pose a threat to our economy, our government, and our civil society.

Cyber Security Is a Major Goal

Governments and citizens must have confidence that the networks at the core of their national security and economic prosperity are safe and resilient. Now this is about more than petty hackers who deface websites. Our ability to bank online, use electronic commerce, and safeguard billions of dollars in intellectual property are all at stake if we cannot rely on the security of our information networks.

Disruptions in these systems demand a coordinated response by all governments, the private sector, and the international community. We need more tools to help law enforcement agencies cooperate across jurisdictions when criminal hackers and organized crime syndicates attack networks for financial gain. The same is true when social ills such as child pornography and the exploitation of trafficked women and girls online is there for the world to see and for those who exploit these people to make a profit. We applaud efforts such as the Council of Europe's Convention on Cybercrime that facilitate international cooperation in prosecuting such offenses. And we wish to redouble our efforts.

We have taken steps as a government . . . to find diplomatic solutions to strengthen global cybersecurity. We have a lot of people in the State Department working on this. They've joined together, and we created two years ago an office to co-ordinate foreign policy in cyberspace. We've worked to address this challenge at the UN [United Nations] and in other multi-lateral forums and to put cybersecurity on the world's agenda. And President Obama has just appointed a new national cyberspace policy coordinator who will help us work even more closely to ensure that everyone's networks stay free, secure, and reliable.

States, terrorists, and those who would act as their proxies must know that the United States will protect our networks. Those who disrupt the free flow of information in our society or any other pose a threat to our economy, our government, and our civil society. Countries or individuals that engage in cyber attacks should face consequences and international condemnation. In an Internet-connected world, an attack on one nation's networks can be an attack on all. And by reinforcing that message, we can create norms of behavior among states and encourage respect for the global networked commons.

The Freedom to Connect Is Transformational

The final freedom, one that was probably inherent in what both President and Mrs. Roosevelt thought about and wrote about all those years ago, is one that flows from the four I've already mentioned: the freedom to connect—the idea that governments should not prevent people from connecting to the Internet, to websites, or to each other. The freedom to connect is like the freedom of assembly, only in cyberspace. It allows individuals to get online, come together, and hopefully cooperate. Once you're on the Internet, you don't need to be a tycoon or a rock star to have a huge impact on society.

The largest public response to the terrorist attacks in Mumbai [India] was launched by a 13-year-old boy. He used social networks to organize blood drives and a massive interfaith book of condolence. In Colombia, an unemployed engineer brought together more than 12 million people in 190 cities around the world to demonstrate against the FARC terrorist movement. The protests were the largest antiterrorist demonstrations in history. And in the weeks that followed, the FARC saw more demobilizations and desertions than it had during a decade of military action. And in Mexico, a single e-mail from a private citizen who was fed up with drug-related violence snowballed into huge demonstrations in all of the country's 32 states. In Mexico City alone, 150,000 people took to the streets in protest. So the Internet can help humanity push back against those who promote violence and crime and extremism.

Our foreign policy is premised on the idea that no country more than America stands to benefit when there is cooperation among peoples and states.

In Iran and Moldova and other countries, online organizing has been a critical tool for advancing democracy and enabling citizens to protest suspicious election results. And even in established democracies like the United States, we've seen the power of these tools to change history. Some of you may still remember the 2008 presidential election here.

The freedom to connect to these technologies can help transform societies, but it is also critically important to individuals. I was recently moved by the story of a doctor—and I won't tell you what country he was from—who was desperately trying to diagnose his daughter's rare medical condition. He consulted with two dozen specialists, but he still didn't have an answer. But he finally identified the condition, and found a cure, by using an Internet search engine. That's one of the reasons why unfettered access to search engine technology is so important in individuals' lives.

The State Department Is Providing
Resources to Protect Internet Freedom

Now, the principles I've outlined today will guide our approach in addressing the issue of Internet freedom and the use of these technologies. And I want to speak about how we apply them in practice. The United States is committed to devoting the diplomatic, economic, and technological resources necessary to advance these freedoms. We are a nation made up of immigrants from every country and every interest that spans the globe. Our foreign policy is premised on the idea that no country more than America stands to benefit when there is cooperation among peoples and states. And no country shoulders a heavier burden when conflict and misunderstanding drive nations apart. So we are well placed to seize the opportunities that come with interconnectivity. And as the birthplace for so many of these technologies, including the Internet itself, we have a responsibility to see them used for good. To do that, we need to develop our capacity for what we call, at the State Department, 21st-century statecraft.

> *Both the American people and nations that censor the Internet should understand that our government is committed to helping promote Internet freedom.*

Realigning our policies and our priorities will not be easy. But adjusting to new technology rarely is. When the telegraph was introduced, it was a source of great anxiety for many in the diplomatic community, where the prospect of receiving daily instructions from capitals was not entirely welcome. But just as our diplomats eventually mastered the telegraph, they are doing the same to harness the potential of these new tools as well.

And I'm proud that the State Department is already working in more than 40 countries to help individuals silenced by oppressive governments. We are making this issue a priority at the United Nations as well, and we're including Internet freedom as a component in the first resolution we introduced after returning to the United Nations Human Rights Council.

We are also supporting the development of new tools that enable citizens to exercise their rights of free expression by circumventing politically motivated censorship. We are providing funds to groups around the world to make sure that those tools get to the people who need them in local languages, and with the training they need to access the Internet safely. The United States has been assisting in these efforts for some time, with a focus on implementing these programs as efficiently and effectively as possible. Both the American people and nations that censor the Internet should understand that our government is committed to helping promote Internet freedom.

We want to put these tools in the hands of people who will use them to advance democracy and human rights, to fight climate change and epidemics, to build global support for President Obama's goal of a world without nuclear weapons, to encourage sustainable economic development that lifts the people at the bottom up.

That's why today I'm announcing that over the next year, we will work with partners in industry, academia, and nongovernmental organizations to establish a standing effort that will harness the power of connection technologies and apply them to our diplomatic goals. By relying on mobile phones, mapping applications, and other new tools, we can empower citizens and leverage our traditional diplomacy. We can address deficiencies in the current market for innovation.

Repressive Governments Should Be Pressured to Have an Open Internet

Lucie Morillon and Jean-François Julliard

Lucie Morillon is head of the new media desk and Jean-François Julliard is secretary-general of Reporters Without Borders.

In authoritarian countries in which the traditional media are state-controlled, the Internet offers a unique space for discussion and information sharing, and has become an ever more important engine for protest and mobilization. The Internet is the crucible in which repressed civil societies can revive and develop.

The new media, and particularly social networks, have given populations collaborative tools with which they can change the social order. Young people have taken them by storm. Facebook has become the rallying point for activists prevented from demonstrating in the streets. One simple video on YouTube—Neda in Iran or the Saffron march of the monks in Burma—can help to expose government abuses to the entire world. One simple USB flash drive can be all it takes to disseminate news—as in Cuba, where they have become the local "samizdats" [term used in the former Soviet Union referring to government-censored publications].

Here, economic interest are intertwined with the need to defend free circulation of information. In some countries, it is companies that have obtained better access to the Internet and to the new media, sometimes with positive consequences for the rest of the population. As a barrier to trade, web censorship should be included on the agenda of the World Trade

Organization. Several of the latter's members, including China and Vietnam, should be required to open their Internet networks before being invited to join the global village of international commerce.

Takeover by Repressive Governments

Yet times have changed since the Internet and the new media were the exclusive province of dissidents and opponents. The leaders of certain countries have been taken aback by a proliferation of new technologies and even more by the emergence of a new form of public debate. They had to suddenly cope with the fact that "Colored Revolutions" had become "Twitter Revolutions." The vast potential of cyberspace can no longer be reserved for dissenting voices. Censoring political and social content with the latest technological tools by arresting and harassing netizens, using omnipresent surveillance and ID registration which compromise surfer anonymity—repressive governments are acting on their threats. In 2009, some sixty countries experienced a form of web censorship, which is twice as many as in 2008. The World Wide Web is being progressively devoured by the implementation of national Intranets whose content is "approved" by the authorities. UzNet, Chinternet, TurkmeNNet ... it does not matter to those governments if more and more Internet users are going to become victims of a digital segregation. Web 2.0 is colliding with Control 2.0

A few rare countries such as North Korea, Burma and Turkmenistan can afford to completely cut themselves off from the World Wide Web. They are not acting on their lack of infrastructure development because it serves their purpose, and it persists. Nonetheless, the telecom black market is prospering in Cuba and on the border between China and North Korea.

Netizens are being targeted at a growing rate. For the first time since the creation of the Internet, a record number of close to 120 bloggers, Internet users and cyber dissidents are behind bars for having expressed themselves freely online. The world's largest netizen prison is in China, which is far out ahead of other countries with 72 detainees, followed by Vietnam and then by Iran, which have all launched waves of brutal attacks on websites in recent months.

The outcome of the cyber-war between netizens and repressive authorities will . . . depend upon the effectiveness of the weapons each camp has available.

Some countries have been arresting netizens in the last few months, even though they have not yet pursued an elaborate Net control or repression strategy. In Morocco, a blogger and a cybercafé owner were jailed by local authorities trying to cover up a crackdown on a demonstration that turned awry. In Azerbaijan, the regime is holding Adnan Hadjizade and Emin Milli—two bloggers who had exposed the corruption of certain officials and had ridiculed them in a video circulated on YouTube. Four online journalists are also behind bars in Yemen. It is too soon to tell if these arrests may herald a new media takeover.

More and more states are enacting or considering repressive laws pertaining to the web, or are applying those that already exist, which is the case with Jordan, Kazakhstan, and Iraq. Western democracies are not immune from the Net regulation trend. In the name of the fight against child pornography or the theft of intellectual property, laws and decrees have been adopted, or are being deliberated, notably in Australia, France, Italy and Great Britain. On a global scale, the Anti-Counterfeiting Trade Agreement (ACTA), whose aim is to fight counterfeiting, is being negotiated behind closed doors, without consulting NGOs [nongovernmental organizations] and civil society. It could possibly introduce potentially liberticidal measures such as the option to implement a filtering system without a court decision.

Some Scandinavian countries are taking a different direction. In Finland, Order no. 732/2009, states that Internet access is a fundamental right for all citizens. By virtue of this text, every Finnish household will have at least a 1 MB/s connection by July 31, 2010. By 2015, it will be at least 100 MB/s. Iceland's Parliament is currently examining a bill, the "Icelandic Modern Media Initiative" (IMMI), which is aimed at strictly protecting freedoms on the Internet by guaranteeing the transparency and independence of information. If it is adopted, Iceland will become a cyber-paradise for bloggers and citizen journalists.

The Internet Users' Response

The outcome of the cyber-war between netizens and repressive authorities will also depend upon the effectiveness of the weapons each camp has available: powerful filtering and surveillance systems for decrypting e-mails, and ever more sophisticated proxies and censorship circumvention tools such as Tor, VPNs, Psiphon, and UltraReach. The latter are developed mainly thanks to the solidarity of netizens around the globe. For example, thousands of Iranians use proxies originally intended for Chinese surfers.

Global pressure makes a difference, too. The major world powers' geostrategic interests are finding a communications platform on the web. In January 2010, the United States made freedom of expression on the Internet the number one goal of its foreign policy. It remains to be seen how the country will apply this strategy to its foreign relations, and what the reaction of the countries concerned will be.

In their apparent isolation, web users, dissidents and bloggers are vulnerable. They are therefore starting to organize, collectively or individually, depending upon what causes they wish to defend. This type of momentum can produce a Russian blogger association, or one comprised of Moroccans, or Belarus web user groups launching campaigns to protest against government decisions, or an Egyptian blogger group mobilizing against torture or the cost of living, or even Chinese Internet users organizing cyber-movements on behalf of Iranian demonstrators on Twitter. Whether their causes are national or global, the messages they communicate are the ones that will decide the landscape of tomorrow's Internet. Resistance is getting organized.

The Enemies of the Internet 2010

The "Enemies of the Internet" list drawn up again this year by Reporters Without Borders presents the worst violators of freedom of expression on the Net: Saudi Arabia, Burma, China, North Korea, Cuba, Egypt, Iran, Uzbekistan, Syria, Tunisia, Turkmenistan, and Vietnam.

Some of these countries are determined to use any means necessary to prevent their citizens from having access to the Internet: Burma, North Korea, Cuba, and Turkmenistan— countries in which technical and financial obstacles are coupled with harsh crackdowns and the existence of a very limited Intranet. Internet shutdowns or major slowdowns are commonplace in periods of unrest. The Internet's potential as a portal open to the world directly contradicts the propensity of these regimes to isolate themselves from other countries. Saudi Arabia and Uzbekistan have opted for such massive filtering that their Internet users have chosen to practice self-censorship. For economic purposes, China, Egypt, Tunisia and Vietnam have wagered on an infrastructure development strategy while keeping a tight control over the web's political and social content (Chinese and Tunisian filtering systems are becoming increasingly sophisticated), and they are demonstrating a deep intolerance for critical opinions. The serious domestic crisis that Iran has been experiencing for months now has caught netizens and the new media in its net; they have become enemies of the regime.

Among the countries "under surveillance" are several democracies: Australia, because of the upcoming implementation of a highly developed Internet filtering system, and South Korea, where draconian laws are creating too many specific restrictions on web users by challenging their anonymity and promoting self-censorship.

Turkey and Russia have just been added to the "Under Surveillance" list. In Russia, aside from the control exercised by the Kremlin on most of its media outlets, the Internet has become the freest space for sharing information. Yet its independence is being jeopardized by blogger arrests and prosecutions, as well as by blockings of so-called "extremist" websites. The regime's propaganda is increasingly omnipresent on the web. There is a real risk that the Internet will be transformed into a tool for political control.

In Turkey, taboo topics mainly deal with [the first president of Turkey, Mustafa Kemal] Ataturk, the army, issues concerning minorities (notably Kurds and Armenians) and the dignity of the Nation. They have served as justification for blocking several thousand sites, including YouTube, thereby triggering a great deal of protest. Bloggers and netizens who express themselves freely on such topics may well face judicial reprisals.

Other countries, such as the United Arab Emirates, Belarus and Thailand are also maintaining their "under surveillance" status, but will need to make more progress to avoid getting transferred into the next "Enemies of the Internet" list. Thailand, because of abuses related to the crime of "lèse-majesté"; the Emirates, because they have bolstered their filtering system; Belarus because its president has just signed a liberticidal order that will regulate the Net, and which will enter into force this summer—just a few months before the elections.

Facebook Should Not Censor Radical Posts

Greg Butterfield

Greg Butterfield is a contributing editor to Workers World.

The U.S.-based social-networking monolith Facebook has begun an all-out assault on its members, deleting three active groups that advocated for progressive and radical causes, permanently banning the accounts of four individuals who administered one group, and sending threatening messages to others.

Facebook Censors Leftist Groups

The groups deleted include Boycott BP, a campaign against the Big Oil company responsible for one of history's worst ecological disasters; the PFLP Solidarity Group, based in New Zealand with members around the globe, in support of the Palestinian resistance movement; and Free Ricardo Palmera!, a group advocating support for a leftist Colombian guerrilla leader who is imprisoned in the U.S. in violation of international law.

Facebook is carrying out its censorship campaign against the left under cover of its arbitrary "terms of service."

Josh Sykes, administrator of the deleted Free Ricardo Palmera! group, received this message: "The group Free Ricardo Palmera! has been removed because it violated our Terms of Use. Among other things, groups that are hateful, threatening, or obscene are not allowed. We also take down groups that attack an individual or group, or advertise a product or service. Continued misuse of Facebook's features could result in your account being disabled."

None of the affected groups was hateful, threatening or obscene in any way. And as anyone who is familiar with Facebook knows, truly hateful, racist, anti-Muslim, anti-women, anti-gay, pro-cop, pro-imperialist and pro-Zionist apartheid groups abound and their members post freely.

Marika Pratley, PFLP Solidarity Campaign coordinator and group administrator, said, "This was clearly a political attack against the PFLP and an attempt by Facebook to censor and shut down the solidarity campaign.

"The PFLP advocates a single secular state in all of Palestine, with equal rights for all, regardless of race or religion, and is the second largest group in the PLO [Palestine Liberation Organization]. Facebook has deemed that support for the PFLP violates its terms and conditions while allowing many blatantly racist anti-Palestinian groups to continue to exist without such censorship."

Facebook is well-known for invasions of personal privacy, but it also has a reputation for censoring leftist causes and national liberation movements. Since 2008, pages and groups supporting Cuba have sometimes been deleted without warning, including one administered by this writer. My personal account was also temporarily suspended.

Another Cuba supporter, an Egyptian-born student activist living outside the U.S., had her account permanently banned. So did a Palestinian student activist from New Jersey whose pro-Palestine liberation group was deleted.

While Facebook is notorious for making its members' personal information available to U.S. corporations, police agencies and the U.S. government, it guards its own contact information zealously. Not only do members sign away their right of appeal to Facebook's censors, but it is almost impossible to lodge a protest. Difficult-to-access options that existed a couple of years ago, at the time of the earlier shutdowns, have been removed.

Facebook Promotes Capitalist Causes

The 700,000-member Boycott BP group was restored after a huge public outcry, including coverage on CNN. Facebook now claims the group was disabled "in error."

While this is an important victory—and shows that Facebook can be pushed back—it is a harder road for lesser-known cases like Palmera's or more controversial causes like the Palestinian resistance movement.

It's important to ask, which groups will Facebook target next? Supporters of political prisoners like Mumia Abu-Jamal? Supporters of the Gaza Freedom Flotilla? Opponents of U.S. wars on Afghanistan, Iraq, Korea and Iran? Supporters of the revolutionary movements in Venezuela, the Philippines and Nepal? Abortion rights advocates?

Social networks should belong to the people, not to U.S. corporations.

Facebook may try to cover its censorship of groups like the PFLP Solidarity Campaign by pointing to the terrible June 21 U.S. Supreme Court decision in *Holder v. Humanitarian Law Project*, which criminalizes free speech under material support statutes related to groups the U.S. government falsely deems "terrorist"—including long-standing national liberation movements in Palestine, Lebanon, Colombia, Nepal and the Philippines.

But the fact is, Facebook and other U.S. corporations benefit from and hold enormous sway over the decisions of the Supreme Court—which, like the other branches of U.S. government, exists to preserve and strengthen the rule of capitalists. The bogus and unconstitutional decision of the Supreme Court must not become an excuse to let Facebook and its ilk off the hook.

Social networking sites have expanded to the point where they are an important and necessary component of all sorts of progressive social advocacy, from modest reforms to revolutionary social change. People all over the world rely on them, so it is especially ludicrous for Facebook to impose the rules of U.S. imperialist foreign policy on its members.

Social networks should belong to the people, not to U.S. corporations. Taking the fight to Facebook now is an important step in that direction.

Censorship Is Appropriate in the Context of Different Value Systems

Derek Bambauer

Derek Bambauer teaches Internet law and intellectual property at the Brooklyn Law School. He also writes Info/Law, *a blog addressing online legal issues.*

Rhetorically, everyone supports Internet freedom. "Freedom," though, means quite different things, and carries diverse weights when measured against other interests in various countries and cultures. This normative divergence plays out in debates over access, threats to freedom, online content controls, and governance. In short, the concept of "Internet freedom" holds within it a set of conflicts about how the Net should function. Acknowledging openly these tensions is better than clinging to wording that masks inevitable, hard choices.

Countries Define Internet Freedom Differently

First, access to the network is a prerequisite for enjoying Internet freedom, however defined. States differ, though, on whether individuals are *entitled* to that access. Some see Internet access—particularly high-speed broadband access—as a right, while others conceive it as a privilege. Finland, for example, has stated that having a 1MB connection is a basic human right of Finnish citizens. Similarly, France's Constitutional Council declared that Internet access is a legal right. The United States, by contrast, views the ability to go online as a market good like any other, rather than seeing it as an en-

Derek Bambauer, "The Enigma of Internet Freedom," Bureau of International Information Programs, U.S. Department of State, July 1, 2010. www.america.gov.

titlement. If you can't afford to connect to the Net, you remain off-line, or dependent on publicly available access sites at libraries and schools.

Whether Internet access is treated as a right or a privilege also holds implications for loss of that access. The United Kingdom's new Digital Economy Act sets up a "graduated response" system that would suspend users' accounts if they are repeatedly accused of online copyright infringement. France's HADOPI (French acronym for the nation's law promoting the distribution and protection of creative works on the Internet) regime similarly disconnects users after three allegations of infringement. Thus, even states that establish access as a right balance it against other considerations, such as protecting intellectual property owners. That balancing act is the key to differing conceptions of Internet freedom.

Countries not only differ on what constitutes Internet freedom, they also diverge on how it should be achieved in practice.

Second, societies vary on the orientation of Internet freedom—in short, free from whom, or from what? One key threat is government. States can impinge online liberties in numerous ways, such as by criminalizing speech or conduct, by monitoring communications, or by blocking material. American views on freedom are typically concerned foremost with preventing unchecked government power. But there are other threats as well. For example, European countries are often wary of the power of corporations to gather private, personally identifiable information about users. Recent controversies over Facebook's privacy settings, Google's video service in Italy, and Google's Street View geo-mapping project demonstrate the worry over remaining free from private sector data gathering as well as governmental surveillance.

In addition, countries may seek to prevent impingements on one's freedom generated by other users—for example, the harm to one's reputation that occurs from false and defamatory content. Some states press intermediaries such as Internet service providers and social networking sites to police this kind of material via the threat of liability, while others provide immunity for anyone but the author. Countries thus demonstrate a range of concerns about threats to freedom.

Third, nations balance differently freedom of expression, and access to information, against concerns about the harms that online material can cause. Those harms can be to individuals (as with defamation), to identifiable groups such as religious or ethnic minorities, or even to shared societal values. The United States views the free exchange of information as sufficiently weighty to displace many competing concerns, which is why material such as hate speech and pornography is protected by its constitution. However, U.S. law does prohibit certain types of information, such as true threats, obscene materials, and child pornography. France and Germany also strongly protect open expression, but ban hate speech online. For example, the countries require Google to filter hate speech sites from its search results on its local language sites. Singapore formally bans pornographic content online, and blocks users from a small set of such sites as a symbolic measure. Saudi Arabia, a country where the majority of citizens are followers of the Sunni branch of Islam, prevents access to certain religious content contrary to Sunni beliefs, such as sites on the Baha'i faith or on the Shia branch of Islam. In short, if we view Internet freedom as protecting unfettered expression, this liberty is counterbalanced to varying degrees by competing concerns, even in countries with strong traditions for protecting speech.

Lastly, countries differ on who should govern Internet freedom, and how it should be implemented. Debates over Internet governance are nearly as old as the commercial Net itself. The United States created the Internet's initial architecture, and retains a baseline level of control over its workings through the relationship between the Department of Commerce and ICANN (the Internet Corporation for Assigned Names and Numbers), which runs the Domain Name System among other tasks. The United States has resisted transfer of ICANN's functions to other entities based, in part, on a concern that placing the Internet under international control would weaken freedom—in particular, freedom of expression. Other states, though, seek a greater voice in decision making about the Net's underlying protocols and standards, and do not want the network to be locked into American conceptions of the proper balance among demands such as security, privacy, and open expression. This has led to heated debate in fora such as the World Summit on the Information Society (WSIS) and to the creation of consultative bodies such as the Internet Governance Forum (IGF). Thus, countries not only differ on what constitutes Internet freedom, they also diverge on how it should be achieved in practice.

A Society's Underlying Values Should Be Respected

Freedom is a loaded term. It holds rhetorical power; portraying one's opponents as averse to Internet freedom is a potent tactic. What makes Internet freedom a difficult goal to achieve is that adherents employ the same term for a range of meanings. Freedom can be conceived of as strongly individualistic, where users are free to act as they please so long as they do not directly harm others. Or, it can be viewed as community-based, where privileges depend upon compliance with a societal framework of rules and norms. Freedom can shield us from interference by states, by companies, and by each other. It can dictate that we have a right to go online, or that we have the opportunity to do so. Internet freedom is thus a dependent term: Its meaning varies with context.

This mutability carries risk, though. Governments may argue that their societies have an understanding of Internet freedom that justifies certain actions while, in fact, those steps are for the benefit of the governing, not the governed. Vietnam, for example, blocks access to certain online material based putatively on concerns about exposure of minors to unhealthy material such as pornography. Yet, the state's system prevents users from reaching sites on human rights and political dissent, while failing to block even a single pornographic page. Plainly, Vietnam's government is engaged in pre-textual behavior. We should be alert to the risk that states will employ legitimate differences about the normative content of "freedom" online as a cover for activities that undermine that liberty.

Perhaps, in the end, Internet freedom is a term that should be abandoned as too general to be useful. Instead, countries, cultures, and users should grapple with the difficult trade-offs that Internet communication presents. The Net empowers pamphleteering as well as pornography. Anonymous communication can be used to inform about political corruption and to infringe intellectual property untraceably. Data aggregation can personalize one's online experience, or profile one's communication and activities. Being explicit about the compromises we make, and being respectful of the underlying values that drive those decisions, will serve us better than using "Internet freedom" to build a false sense of consensus.

The US Insistence on Internet Freedom Does More Harm than Good

Clay Shirky

Clay Shirky is professor of new media at New York University and the author of Cognitive Surplus: Creativity and Generosity *in a Connected Age.*

On January 17, 2001, during the impeachment trial of Philippine President Joseph Estrada, loyalists in the Philippine Congress voted to set aside key evidence against him. Less than two hours after the decision was announced, thousands of Filipinos, angry that their corrupt president might be let off the hook, converged on Epifanio de los Santos Avenue, a major crossroads in Manila. The protest was arranged, in part, by forwarded text messages reading, "Go 2 EDSA. Wear blk." The crowd quickly swelled, and in the next few days, over a million people arrived, choking traffic in downtown Manila.

The public's ability to coordinate such a massive and rapid response—close to seven million text messages were sent that week—so alarmed the country's legislators that they reversed course and allowed the evidence to be presented. Estrada's fate was sealed; by January 20, he was gone. The event marked the first time that social media had helped force out a national leader. Estrada himself blamed "the text-messaging generation" for his downfall.

Social Media Has a Mixed Record

Since the rise of the Internet in the early 1990s, the world's networked population has grown from the low millions to the low billions. Over the same period, social media have become a fact of life for civil society worldwide, involving many actors—regular citizens, activists, nongovernmental organizations, telecommunications firms, software providers, governments. This raises an obvious question for the U.S. government: How does the ubiquity of social media affect U.S. interests, and how should U.S. policy respond to it?

As the communications landscape gets denser, more complex, and more participatory, the networked population is gaining greater access to information, more opportunities to engage in public speech, and an enhanced ability to undertake collective action. In the political arena, as the protests in Manila demonstrated, these increased freedoms can help loosely coordinated publics demand change.

Attempts to yoke the idea of Internet freedom to short-term goals . . . are likely to be ineffective on average.

The Philippine strategy has been adopted many times since. In some cases, the protesters ultimately succeeded, as in Spain in 2004, when demonstrations organized by text messaging led to the quick ouster of Spanish Prime Minister José María Aznar, who had inaccurately blamed the Madrid transit bombings on Basque separatists. . . .

There are, however, many examples of the activists failing, as in Belarus in March 2006, when street protests (arranged in part by e-mail) against President Aleksandr Lukashenko's alleged vote rigging swelled, then faltered, leaving Lukashenko more determined than ever to control social media. . . .

The use of social media tools—text messaging, e-mail, photo sharing, social networking, and the like—does not have a single preordained outcome. Therefore, attempts to outline their effects on political action are too often reduced to dueling anecdotes. . . .

Despite this mixed record, social media have become coordinating tools for nearly all of the world's political movements, just as most of the world's authoritarian governments (and, alarmingly, an increasing number of democratic ones) are trying to limit access to it. In response, the U.S. State Department has committed itself to "Internet freedom" as a specific policy aim. Arguing for the right of people to use the Internet freely is an appropriate policy for the United States, both because it aligns with the strategic goal of strengthening civil society worldwide and because it resonates with American beliefs about freedom of expression. But attempts to yoke the idea of Internet freedom to short-term goals—particularly ones that are country-specific or are intended to help particular dissident groups or encourage regime change—are likely to be ineffective on average. And when they fail, the consequences can be serious.

The instrumental view [of Internet freedom articulated by US Secretary of State Hillary Clinton] is politically appealing, action-oriented, and almost certainly wrong.

Although the story of Estrada's ouster and other similar events have led observers to focus on the power of mass protests to topple governments, the potential of social media lies mainly in their support of civil society and the public sphere—change measured in years and decades rather than weeks or months. The U.S. government should maintain Internet freedom as a goal to be pursued in a principled and regime-neutral fashion, not as a tool for effecting immediate policy aims country by country. It should likewise assume that progress will be incremental and, unsurprisingly, slowest in the most authoritarian regimes.

The Perils of Internet Freedom

In January 2010, U.S. Secretary of State Hillary Clinton outlined how the United States would promote Internet freedom abroad. She emphasized several kinds of freedom, including the freedom to access information (such as the ability to use Wikipedia and Google inside Iran), the freedom of ordinary citizens to produce their own public media (such as the rights of Burmese activists to blog), and the freedom of citizens to converse with one another (such as the Chinese public's capacity to use instant messaging without interference).

Most notably, Clinton announced funding for the development of tools designed to reopen access to the Internet in countries that restrict it. This "instrumental" approach to Internet freedom concentrates on preventing states from censoring outside websites, such as Google, YouTube, or that of the *New York Times*. It focuses only secondarily on public speech by citizens and least of all on private or social uses of digital media. According to this vision, Washington can and should deliver rapid, directed responses to censorship by authoritarian regimes.

The instrumental view is politically appealing, action-oriented, and almost certainly wrong. It overestimates the value of broadcast media while underestimating the value of media that allow citizens to communicate privately among themselves. It overestimates the value of access to information, particularly information hosted in the West, while underestimating the value of tools for local coordination. And it overestimates the importance of computers while underestimating the importance of simpler tools, such as cell phones.

The instrumental approach can also be dangerous. Consider the debacle around the proposed censorship-circumvention software known as Haystack, which, according to its developer, was meant to be a "one-to-one match for how the [Iranian] regime implements censorship." The tool was widely praised in Washington; the U.S. government even granted it an export license. But the program was never carefully vetted, and when security experts examined it, it turned out that it not only failed at its goal of hiding messages from governments but also made it, in the words of one analyst, "possible for an adversary to specifically pinpoint individual users." In contrast, one of the most successful anticensorship software programs, Freegate, has received little support from the United States, partly because of ordinary bureaucratic delays and partly because the U.S. government is wary of damaging U.S.-Chinese relations: the tool was originally created by Falun Gong, the spiritual movement that the Chinese government has called "an evil cult." The challenges of Freegate and Haystack demonstrate how difficult it is to weaponize social media to pursue country-specific and near-term policy goals.

The more promising way to think about social media is as long-term tools that can strengthen civil society and the public sphere.

New media conducive to fostering participation can indeed increase the freedoms Clinton outlined, just as the printing press, the postal service, the telegraph, and the telephone did before. One complaint about the idea of new media as a political force is that most people simply use these tools for commerce, social life, or self-distraction, but this is common to all forms of media. Far more people in the 1500s were reading erotic novels than Martin Luther's "Ninety-Five Theses," and far more people before the American Revolution were reading *Poor Richard's Almanack* than the work of the Committees of Correspondence. But those political works still had an enormous political effect.

Just as Luther adopted the newly practical printing press to protest against the Catholic Church, and the American revolutionaries synchronized their beliefs using the postal service that Benjamin Franklin had designed, today's dissident movements will use any means possible to frame their views and coordinate their actions; it would be impossible to describe the Moldovan Communist Party's loss of Parliament after the 2009 elections without discussing the use of cell phones and online tools by its opponents to mobilize. Authoritarian governments stifle communication among their citizens because they fear, correctly, that a better-coordinated populace would constrain their ability to act without oversight.

Despite this basic truth—that communicative freedom is good for political freedom—the instrumental mode of Internet statecraft is still problematic. It is difficult for outsiders to understand the local conditions of dissent. External support runs the risk of tainting even peaceful opposition as being directed by foreign elements. Dissidents can be exposed by the unintended effects of novel tools. A government's demands for Internet freedom abroad can vary from country to country, depending on the importance of the relationship, leading to cynicism about its motives.

The more promising way to think about social media is as long-term tools that can strengthen civil society and the public sphere. In contrast to the instrumental view of Internet freedom, this can be called the "environmental" view. According to this conception, positive changes in the life of a country, including pro-democratic regime change, follow, rather than precede, the development of a strong public sphere. This is not to say that popular movements will not successfully use these tools to discipline or even oust their governments, but rather that U.S. attempts to direct such uses are likely to do more harm than good. Considered in this light, Internet freedom is a long game, to be conceived of and supported not as a separate agenda but merely as an important input to the more fundamental political freedoms. . . .

The Theater of Collapse

Political freedom has to be accompanied by a civil society literate enough and densely connected enough to discuss the issues presented to the public. In a famous study of political opinion after the 1948 U.S. presidential election, the sociologists Elihu Katz and Paul Lazarsfeld discovered that mass media alone do not change people's minds; instead, there is a two-step process. Opinions are first transmitted by the media, and then they get echoed by friends, family members, and colleagues. It is in this second, social step that political opinions are formed. This is the step in which the Internet in general, and social media in particular, can make a difference. As with the printing press, the Internet spreads not just media consumption but media production as well—it allows people to privately and publicly articulate and debate a welter of conflicting views.

A slowly developing public sphere, where public opinion relies on both media and conversation, is the core of the environmental view of Internet freedom. As opposed to the self-aggrandizing view that the West holds the source code for democracy—and if it were only made accessible, the remaining autocratic states would crumble—the environmental view assumes that little political change happens without the dissemination and adoption of ideas and opinions in the public sphere. Access to information is far less important, politically, than access to conversation. Moreover, a public sphere is more likely to emerge in a society as a result of people's dissatisfaction with matters of economics or day-to-day governance than from their embrace of abstract political ideals.

To take a contemporary example, the Chinese government today is in more danger of being forced to adopt democratic norms by middle-class members of the ethnic Han majority demanding less corrupt local governments than it is by Uighurs or Tibetans demanding autonomy. Similarly, the One Million Signatures Campaign, an Iranian women's rights movement that focuses on the repeal of laws inimical to women, has been more successful in liberalizing the behavior of the Iranian government than the more confrontational Green Movement.

For optimistic observers of public demonstrations, this is weak tea, but both the empirical and the theoretical work suggest that protests, when effective, are the end of a long process, rather than a replacement for it. Any real commitment by the United States to improving political freedom worldwide should concentrate on that process—which can only occur when there is a strong public sphere. . . .

Social Media Skepticism

There are, broadly speaking, two arguments against the idea that social media will make a difference in national politics. The first is that the tools are themselves ineffective, and the second is that they produce as much harm to democratization as good, because repressive governments are becoming better at using these tools to suppress dissent.

The critique of ineffectiveness, most recently offered by Malcolm Gladwell in the *New Yorker*, concentrates on examples of what has been termed "slacktivism," whereby casual participants seek social change through low-cost activities, such as joining Facebook's "Save Darfur" group, that are long on bumper-sticker sentiment and short on any useful action. The critique is correct but not central to the question of social media's power; the fact that barely committed actors cannot click their way to a better world does not mean that committed actors cannot use social media effectively. Recent protest movements—including a movement against fundamentalist vigilantes in India in 2009, the beef protests in South Korea in 2008, and protests against education laws in Chile in 2006—have used social media not as a replacement for real-world action but as a way to coordinate it. As a result, all of those protests exposed participants to the threat of violence, and in some cases its actual use. In fact, the adoption of these tools (especially cell phones) as a way to coordinate and document real-world action is so ubiquitous that it will probably be a part of all future political movements.

This obviously does not mean that every political movement that uses these tools will succeed, because the state has not lost the power to react. This points to the second, and much more serious, critique of social media as tools for political improvement—namely, that the state is gaining increasingly sophisticated means of monitoring, interdicting, or co-opting these tools. The use of social media, the scholars Rebecca MacKinnon of the New America Foundation and Evgeny Morozov of the Open Society Institute have argued, is just as likely to strengthen authoritarian regimes as it is to weaken them. The Chinese government has spent considerable effort perfecting several systems for controlling political threats from social media. The least important of these is its censorship and surveillance program. Increasingly, the government recognizes that threats to its legitimacy are coming from inside the state and that blocking the website of the *New York Times* does little to prevent grieving mothers from airing their complaints about corruption.

> *To the degree that the United States pursues Internet freedom as a tool of statecraft, it should de-emphasize anticensorship tools . . . and increase its support for local public speech and assembly.*

The Chinese system has evolved from a relatively simple filter of incoming Internet traffic in the mid-1990s to a sophisticated operation that not only limits outside information but also uses arguments about nationalism and public morals to encourage operators of Chinese web services to censor their users and users to censor themselves. Because its goal is to prevent information from having politically synchronizing effects, the state does not need to censor the Internet comprehensively; rather, it just needs to minimize access to information.

Authoritarian states are increasingly shutting down their communications grids to deny dissidents the ability to coordinate in real time and broadcast documentation of an event.

This strategy also activates the conservative dilemma, creating a short-term risk of alerting the population at large to political conflict. When the government of Bahrain banned Google Earth after an annotated map of the royal family's annexation of public land began circulating, the effect was to alert far more Bahrainis to the offending map than knew about it originally. So widely did the news spread that the government relented and reopened access after four days.

Such shutdowns become more problematic for governments if they are long-lived. When antigovernment protesters occupied Bangkok in the summer of 2010, their physical presence disrupted Bangkok's shopping district, but the state's reaction, cutting off significant parts of the Thai telecommunications infrastructure, affected people far from the capital. The approach creates an additional dilemma for the state—there can be no modern economy without working phones—and so its ability to shut down communications over large areas or long periods is constrained.

In the most extreme cases, the use of social media tools is a matter of life and death, as with the proposed death sentence for the blogger Hossein Derakhshan in Iran (since commuted to 19 and a half years in prison) or the suspicious hanging death of Oleg Bebenin, the founder of the Belarusian opposition website Charter 97. Indeed, the best practical reason to think that social media can help bring political change is that both dissidents and governments think they can. All over the world, activists believe in the utility of these tools and take steps to use them accordingly. And the governments they contend with think social media tools are powerful, too, and are willing to harass, arrest, exile, or kill users in response. One way the United States can heighten the conservative dilemma without running afoul of as many political complications is to demand the release of citizens imprisoned for using media in these ways. Anything that constrains the worst threats of violence by the state against citizens using these tools also increases the conservative dilemma.

Looking at the Long Run

To the degree that the United States pursues Internet freedom as a tool of statecraft, it should de-emphasize anticensorship tools, particularly those aimed at specific regimes, and increase its support for local public speech and assembly more generally. Access to information is not unimportant, of course, but it is not the primary way social media constrain autocratic rulers or benefit citizens of a democracy. Direct, U.S. government-sponsored support for specific tools or campaigns targeted at specific regimes risk creating backlash that a more patient and global application of principles will not.

This entails reordering the State Department's Internet freedom goals. Securing the freedom of personal and social communication among a state's population should be the highest priority, closely followed by securing individual citizens' ability to speak in public. This reordering would reflect the reality that it is a strong civil society—one in which citizens have freedom of assembly—rather than access to Google or YouTube, that does the most to force governments to serve their citizens.

As a practical example of this, the United States should be at least as worried about Egypt's recent controls on the mandatory licensing of group-oriented text-messaging services as it is about Egypt's attempts to add new restrictions on press freedom. The freedom of assembly that such text-messaging services support is as central to American democratic ideals as is freedom of the press. Similarly, South Korea's requirement that citizens register with their real names for certain Internet services is an attempt to reduce their ability to surprise the state with the kind of coordinated action that took place during the 2008 protest in Seoul. If the United States does not complain as directly about this policy as it does about Chinese censorship, it risks compromising its ability to argue for Internet freedom as a global ideal.

More difficult, but also essential, will be for the U.S. government to articulate a policy of engagement with the private companies and organizations that host the networked public sphere. Services based in the United States, such as Facebook, Twitter, Wikipedia, and YouTube, and those based overseas, such as QQ (a Chinese instant-messaging service), WikiLeaks (a repository of leaked documents whose servers are in Sweden), Tuenti (a Spanish social network), and Naver (a Korean one), are among the sites used most for political speech, conversation, and coordination. And the world's wireless carriers transmit text messages, photos, and videos from cell phones through those sites. How much can these entities be expected to support freedom of speech and assembly for their users?

The issue here is analogous to the questions about freedom of speech in the United States in private but commercial environments, such as those regarding what kind of protests can be conducted in shopping malls. For good or ill, the platforms supporting the networked public sphere are privately held and run; Clinton committed the United States to working with those companies, but it is unlikely that without some legal framework, as exists for real-world speech and action, moral suasion will be enough to convince commercial actors to support freedom of speech and assembly.

It would be nice to have a flexible set of short-term digital tactics that could be used against different regimes at different times. But the requirements of real-world statecraft mean that what is desirable may not be likely. Activists in both repressive and democratic regimes will use the Internet and related tools to try to effect change in their countries, but Washington's ability to shape or target these changes is limited. Instead, Washington should adopt a more general approach, promoting freedom of speech, freedom of the press, and freedom of assembly everywhere. And it should understand that progress will be slow. Only by switching from an instrumental to an environmental view of the effects of social media on the public sphere will the United States be able to take advantage of the long-term benefits these tools promise—even though that may mean accepting short-term disappointment.

Schools Need to Establish Some Limits to Social Media Use

Kathryn S. Vander Broek, Steven M. Puiszis, and Evan D. Brown

Kathryn S. Vander Broek and Steven M. Puiszis are partners with Hinshaw & Culbertson LLP, and Evan D. Brown is an associate with the firm.

The Internet is a modern-day Pandora's box. It offers a forum "for a true diversity of political discourse, unique opportunities for cultural development, and myriad avenues of intellectual activity." The Internet can provide meaningful learning opportunities for educators and students unimaginable to earlier generations, while raising a host of concerns for school administrators and parents over its appropriate use. Best practice questions abound concerning how to effectively and productively integrate the Internet into the educational setting while simultaneously protecting students.

The Internet has brought to the classroom's door a fundamental paradox confronting our legal and educational systems. Specifically, students using the Internet must be protected from inappropriate content or predatory practices, while the First Amendment protects the rights of those who speak, write, or convey ideas or display symbols over the web. One of the Internet's unfortunate by-products is that in today's digital era, school administrators are being called upon with increasing frequency to balance the use of Internet-based tools that enrich learning against the need to maintain order and a safe learning environment. Balancing these competing concerns is a complex and delicate task. . . .

Kathryn S. Vander Broek, Steven M. Puiszis, and Evan D. Brown, "Schools and Social Media: First Amendment Issues Arising from Student Use of the Internet," *Intellectual Property & Technology Law Journal*, v. 21, no. 4, April 2009, pp. 11–27. Copyright © 2009 by Aspen Publishers Inc. All rights reserved. Reproduced by permission.

School officials are not permitted to prohibit or discipline student speech or expressive activity simply because it may be provocative or controversial, the officials disagree with the student's point of view, or the speech is crude or distasteful. Indeed, one of the core functions of the First Amendment is to protect controversial speech. In a series of decisions highlighted in the following sections, the Supreme Court has attempted to balance these competing principles, and has broadly outlined when a school lawfully can restrict or discipline a student for speech or expressive activity that would otherwise fall within the ambit of the First Amendment.

In order to understand and meaningfully evaluate the types of First Amendment issues that have arisen involving student speech and the Internet, it is important to have a basic understanding of the dynamics of the modern web. These dynamics are shaped by the technological and cultural context in which information is distributed on the web. Much of today's web activity involves the creation and consumption of "social media." This term broadly describes the various ways that Internet users interact with one another online, and comprises such activities as creating and commenting on blogs, uploading and sharing user-generated content, such as video and photos, and communicating with friends through social networking sites such as MySpace or Facebook. Typically, when new members join a social networking site, they design an online profile page, which allows them to communicate with other members through e-mail, instant messaging (IM), or electronic bulletin board postings. A member's online profile can be open to all or access can be limited only to "friends" or "buddies." . . .

Many courts have been slow to focus on the unique characteristics of the Internet that distinguish it from traditional modes of communication. Several of the traditional forms of communication, such as the print and broadcast media, are heavily regulated and expensive to use. Many individuals lack the resources necessary to use these forums. On the other hand, the Internet is both easy and inexpensive to use. Additionally, one of the more attractive features of the web is that it permits the free and unfettered discussion of issues, with practically no regulation or oversight. The spoken or printed word is capable of reaching a finite and limited audience. Information posted on the Internet can instantaneously reach a far larger audience potentially anywhere in the world. Moreover, social networking sites and web-based interactive services encourage the development of affinity groups sharing common interests. As a result, messages can be easily conveyed to persons sharing the same interests or points of view. Anonymity is another feature of the Internet that makes it a preferred mode of communication for many who otherwise may be unwilling to express their views on controversial subject matters. These features make the Internet a highly popular and effective means of communicating ideas and information. However, these same features also make negative comments far more damaging and anonymous messages or threats far more menacing when made over the Internet.

School administrators are being called upon ... to balance the use of Internet-based tools that enrich learning against the need to maintain order and a safe learning environment.

Internet-related student speech decisions have involved a myriad of fact patterns, and a wide variety of social media. The decisions have addressed the creation of phony and offensive MySpace profiles of school officials; web pages containing crude and vulgar language or mock obituaries of other students, a list of persons who the website creator wishes would die, and one with a drawing of a teacher with her head cut off; the use of an instant messaging (IM) icon depicting a teacher being shot; a slide show posted on YouTube dramatizing the murder of a teacher; "trash talking" on website messages boards, and messages broadcast on publicly accessible blogs. For the most part, the students worked online from home, although their intended audience generally was other students at their school.

A number of lower courts, while sympathetic to a school district's need to maintain a safe and orderly learning environment, nevertheless enjoined student discipline for Internet-related speech or statements made on social networking websites originating from the student's home. In several instances, the courts concluded that the speech did not involve a true threat or was not lewd or that it was lewd speech but occurred off campus or that a school's concerns over a potential disruption were overblown. While a few of these decisions can be explained by a failure of proof or by a disagreement over the proper test for determining whether a statement qualifies as a true threat, the reasoning of several of these decisions is difficult to reconcile. . . .

Students and teachers are no different from any other web users in that they stand to benefit from the numerous kinds of tools available to facilitate communication and collaboration. The educational experience can be streamlined, and indeed enhanced, by the use of platforms that make it easier for teachers and students to interact with each other and among themselves. Many of the functions that one sees in the typical social networking site, like messaging, sharing links, and common collaboration spaces, can be used in the school context. Teachers can post assignments and class notes and answer frequently asked questions. Students can send messages to their teachers seeking help on particular issues. . . .

As use of the Internet in school settings expands, some state legislatures are requiring school districts to incorporate Internet safety instruction into the curriculum. In August 2007, for example, the Illinois School Code was amended to afford school districts the opportunity to establish age-appropriate curriculum content in the area of Internet safety education for grades K–12. The purpose of the education was to "inform and protect students from inappropriate or illegal communications and solicitation and to encourage school districts to provide education about Internet threats and risks, including without limitation child predators, fraud, and other dangers." The overriding legislative concern was use of the Internet by sexual predators and deceptive practices that result in harassment, exploitation and physical harm.

Two hours of instruction per year was recommended, to include subjects on:

- Safe and responsible use of social networking websites, chat rooms, electronic mail, bulletin boards, instant messaging, and other means of communication on the Internet;

- Recognizing, avoiding, and reporting online solicitations of students, their classmates, and their friends by sexual predators;

- Risks of transmitting personal information on the Internet;

- Recognizing and avoiding unsolicited or deceptive communications received online;

- Recognizing and reporting online harassment and cyberbullying;

- Reporting illegal activities and communications on the Internet; and

- Copyright laws on written materials, photographs, music, and video. . . .

- Including cyberbullying in your district's definition of bullying gives school administrators a platform from which to impose appropriate consequences for use of social media to intimidate, harass, threaten, or otherwise bully others. Before taking action, you still may need to analyze the nature of the communication(s) to determine if it is protected by First Amendment free speech rights. The failure to incorporate use of the Internet or other forms of social media when defining bullying in the district's discipline code, however, may preclude administrators from lawfully imposing disciplinary consequences for its misuse. . . .

- Be certain your policies and trainings addressing the prohibition of harassment and discrimination include the use of blogs or other social media as a prohibited means for engaging in such conduct for which disciplinary action may be taken.

Organizations to Contact

The editors have compiled the following list of organizations concerned with the issues debated in this book. The descriptions are derived from materials provided by the organizations. All have publications or information available for interested readers. The list was compiled on the date of publication of the present volume; the information provided here may change. Be aware that many organizations take several weeks or longer to respond to inquiries, so allow as much time as possible.

Internet Keep Safe Coalition
1401 K Street NW, Suite 600, Washington, DC   20005
(202) 587-5583 • fax: (202) 737-4097
e-mail: info@iKeepSafe.org
website: www.iKeepSafe.org

The Internet Keep Safe Coalition is a nonprofit organization that teaches basic rules of Internet safety to children and parents. Its website contains material for children, parents, and educators. The coalition publishes books, CDs, and DVDs on Internet safety, including the children's book *Faux Paw's Adventures in the Internet: Keeping Children Safe Online.*

New Media Consortium (NMC)
6101 W. Courtyard, Building One, Suite 100
Austin, TX   78730
(512) 445-4200 • fax: (512) 445-4205
website: www.nmc.org

The New Media Consortium (NMC) is an international consortium of colleges, universities, museums, and research centers dedicated to the exploration and use of new media and new technologies. For more than fifteen years, the consortium and its members have dedicated themselves to exploring and developing potential applications of emerging technologies for learning, research, and creative inquiry.

New Media Institute (NMI)
110 William Street, 22nd Floor, New York, NY   10038
(917) 652-7141
website: www.newmedia.org

The New Media Institute (NMI) is a research and fact-finding organization whose mission is to improve public understanding of issues surrounding the Internet and other forms of new media communications. NMI works directly with the news media, researchers, academics, government, and industry professionals, as well as serving as a primary resource of facts, statistics, and analysis.

Web Wise Kids
PO Box 27203, Santa Ana, CA   92799
(866) WEB-WISE • fax: (714) 435-0523
e-mail: info@webwisekids.org
website: www.webwisekids.org

Web Wise Kids is a nonprofit online safety organization that works with kids, parents, teachers, and law enforcement to protect today's youth from online dangers. The mission of the organization is to help youth make wise choices online.

Bibliography

Books

Victoria Carty   *Wired and Mobilizing: Social Movements, New Technology, and Electoral Politics.* New York: Routledge, 2011.

Rahaf Harfoush   *Yes We Did: An Inside Look at How Social Media Built the Obama Brand.* Berkeley, CA: New Riders, 2009.

John Allen Hendricks and Robert E. Denton Jr., eds.   *Communicator-in-Chief: How Barack Obama Used New Media Technology to Win the White House.* Lanham, MD: Lexington Books, 2010.

Elliot King   *Free for All: The Internet's Transformation of Journalism.* Evanston, IL: Northwestern University Press, 2010.

David Kirkpatrick   *The Facebook Effect: The Inside Story of the Company That Is Connecting the World.* New York: Simon & Schuster, 2010.

Joe Trippi   *The Revolution Will Not Be Televised: Democracy, the Internet, and the Overthrow of Everything.* New York: HarperCollins, 2004.

Sean Tunney and Garrett Monaghan, eds.   *Web Journalism: A New Form of Citizenship?.* Portland, OR: Sussex Academic Press, 2010.

Periodicals and Internet Sources

Philip Alexiou   "A 'Twitter Moment' in Politics?,"
Voice of America, July 29, 2010.
www.voanews.com.

Paul Allen   "Social Media and Elections: The
Revolution Will Not Be Televised,
Revisited," Paulallen.net, September
29, 2009. http://paulallen.net.

Chen Baoguo   "US Controls Threaten Internet
Freedom," *Global Times*, August 23,
2010.

The Economist   "Social Networks and Statehood: The
Future Is Another Country," vol. 396,
no. 8692, July 22, 2010.

Mike Giglio   "The Cyberactivists Who Helped
Topple a Dictator," *Newsweek*,
January 15, 2011.

Wen Guang   "Google Incident and US Internet
Strategy," *China Daily*, January 23,
2010.

Ruth A. Harper   "The Social Media Revolution:
Exploring the Impact on Journalism
and News Media Organizations,"
Student Pulse, March 11, 2010.
www.studentpulse.com.

Peter Kirwan   "From Samizdat to Twitter: How
Technology Is Making Censorship
Irrelevant," *Wired*, August 1, 2010.

Claire Cain Miller "How Obama's Internet Campaign Changed Politics," *New York Times*, November 7, 2008.

Georgianne Nienaber "Call for Social Networking Reports on Deepwater Horizon Oil Impacts," *Huffington Post*, May 4, 2010. www.huffingtonpost.com.

Robert G. Picard "Blogs, Tweets, Social Media, and the News Business," *Neiman Reports*, vol. 63, no. 3, Fall 2009.

Jennifer Preston "Movement Began with Outrage and a Facebook Page That Gave It an Outlet," *New York Times*, February 5, 2011.

Samantha M. Shapiro "Can Social Networking Turn Disaffected Young Egyptians into a Force for Democratic Change?," *New York Times Magazine*, January 25, 2009.

Josh Taylor "Facebook Is Ruining Journalism," *Newsphobia*, January 20, 2009. www.newsphobia.net.

Jose Antonio Vargas "Internet Freedom, Hillary Clinton and Being the Web's First Global Diplomat," *Huffington Post*, January 21, 2010. www.huffingtonpost.com.

David Wills and Stuart Reeves "Facebook as a Political Weapon: Information in Social Networks," *British Politics*, vol. 4, no. 2, June 2009.

Lea Winerman   "Social Networking: Crisis Communication," *Nature*, January 21, 2009. www.nature.com.

Gary Wolf   "How the Internet Invented Howard Dean," *Wired*, January 2004. www.wired.com.

Li Xiguang   "Voices of Online Masses Can Make China Heard Worldwide," *Global Times*, February 22, 2011.

Index

C